THE DIABETIC KITCHEN

THE DIABETIC KITCHEN

Healthy and Tasty Recipes to Keep Your Blood Sugar in Check

VERONICA MILES

peapil

Peapil Publishing (Canada)
304 — 1180 Sunset Drive
Kelowna B.C. V1Y 9W6

Peapil Publishing (United States)
2507 S 300 W
Salt Lake City, Utah 84165
peapilpublishing.com

Library of Congress Cataloging-in-Publication Data

Names: Miles, Veronica, author.
Title: The diabetic kitchen: healthy and tasty recipes to keep your blood
   sugar in check / by Veronica Miles.
Description: First edition. | Kelowna, B.C.; Salt Lake City, Utah: Peapil
   Publishing, [2023]
Identifiers: LCCN 2023039026 (print) | LCCN 2023039027 (ebook) | ISBN
   9781990281709 (hardback) | ISBN 9781990281679 (paperback) | ISBN
   9781990281693 (ebook) | ISBN 9781990281686 (audiobook)
Subjects: LCSH: Diabetes—Diet therapy—Recipes.
Classification: LCC RC662 .M537 2023 (print) | LCC RC662 (ebook) | DDC
   641.5/6314–dc23/eng/20231003
LC record available at https://lccn.loc.gov/2023039026
LC ebook record available at https://lccn.loc.gov/2023039027

Interior by Anna B. Knighton
Cover Design by Andrea Ho
Contributions by Kirsten Armstrong
Photography by David E. Carranza Calvillo
Food Styling by Itze McConnehey

First Edition

Contact the author at support@peapil.com

Paperback ISBN: 978-1-990281-67-9
Hardback ISBN: 978-1-990281-70-9
eBook ISBN: 978-1-990281-69-3
Audiobook ISBN: 978-1-990281-68-6

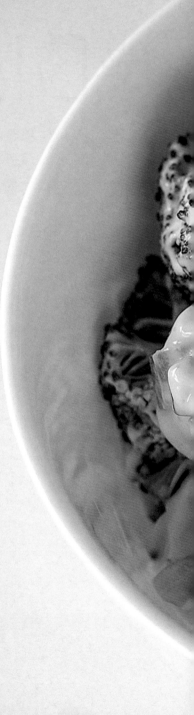

Disclaimer

Contents

Introduction

While my life journey started with all things Mediterranean—the sea, the culture, and the food—my professional journey stemmed from my love of people. I became a life coach to help people find self-love; and I became a chef to help people rediscover the joy of food. To put it simply, my job is to support people in finding a lifestyle that suits their needs. Whether someone has career, self-esteem, mindset, or relationship goals, it all comes down to lifestyle. Honing a lifestyle that inspires you paves the way for the growth you desire.

My first client as a life coach had a goal to gain confidence. Since confidence flows from many facets of life, we progressed through food acceptance, body positivity, leadership skills, and more. It's been over a decade since I introduced myself—and my values—to Jenny. I've now grown an entire business derived from my love of people.

When you show someone love, you support them through growth—and this is where I've made my career. I tailor, adapt, and polish lifestyles for everyone, pushing my clients to be the best versions of themselves. When I find a common thread between my clients' needs, such as the benefits of healthful food like the Mediterranean diet, I cultivate tools to help them even after they no longer need my services. And that is how my previous cookbooks were born.

We're here now because after twelve years, I've seen my fair share of clients with diabetes. And while I was able to help them through the darkest time of their conditions—whether that was diagnosis, acceptance, or understanding—I found that each year the number of my clients with diabetes grew. This makes sense, since according to the National Institute of Health, more than 11 percent of Americans suffer from diabetes. That's 37.3 million people. To put that unrelatable number into perspective, when you gather with your extended family, chances are at least one of you has the chronic condition. Diabetes is pervasive throughout our country, and I'm here to show these individuals love!

The truth is, I didn't consider putting together this cookbook until an unexpected call from my cousin, Lilian.

Last year, I was in the middle of grocery shopping when Lilian's voice broke through my introspective mental chatter with the words "I need help." I sped to her house, threw open the door, and enfolded her in my arms. Then I sat on her couch and said, "Tell me everything."

Lilian's symptoms started small: blurry vision, subtle weight loss, exhaustion, and numbing in her limbs. With three children younger than ten and a husband who travels for work, Lilian pushed her symptoms aside to prioritize her family. That is, until her eyesight became so hazy that she finally caved and made an appointment with her optometrist. After she blatantly failed her standard eye test, one she had aced just a few years earlier, the optometrist ran some tests. Within a few weeks, her family physician and optometrist came to the same conclusion: Lilian had type 2 diabetes, with blurry vision arising from diabetic retinopathy.

What is diabetic retinopathy? While not everyone with diabetes develops it, the condition happens when blood vessels within the retina change, causing leaks or growths. In fact, it is the leading cause of blindness in Americans. Blurry vision can be one of the tell-tale signs for diabetes.

Lilian and I sat together while I listened to one of my closest confidants reveal her deepest fears. Like many of my clients, Lilian's life felt overwhelming and taxing. By the time she finished work, picked up the kids, threw dinner in the oven, and cleaned up, she drifted off in front of the TV. Exercise felt impossible to her. Meal planning felt daunting. And now, conquering her diabetes symptoms felt insurmountable. While a concerning diagnosis, there is one positive aspect: you have the power to make changes.

She felt hopeless, but thankfully, I'm in the business of creating hope. I explained to her that none of the necessary changes would show results within a week, a month, or even a year. A healthy lifestyle is just that—a lifestyle. It takes conscious decisions and deliberate effort every single day. But eventually, one day, she would look back and realize just how distanced she was from where she started.

Lilian's most pressing question—one I've heard many, many times—was, "Where do I start?"

If you or a loved one suffer from diabetes and are hoping to overhaul your lifestyle, this book is crafted for you. Lilian's story is not unique, it's actually extremely common. My devotion to Lilian's story sparked the creation of this cookbook, and I hope this cookbook sparks a change in you!

What Exactly Is Diabetes?

Diabetes comes in three forms: **type 1**, **type 2**, and **gestational**. All three forms affect how your body transforms food into energy.

TYPE 1 DIABETES

Typically known as juvenile or insulin-dependent diabetes, type 1 diabetes occurs when the pancreas produces little or no insulin. Insulin is an essential hormone because it turns food into energy, controlling just how much glucose (sugar) is in your body at any given moment. When you eat food, it becomes sugar as it enters your blood. Insulin's job is to move this sugar from your blood into cells, storing it in your liver, fat, and muscles. Insulin also controls your body's metabolism of carbohydrates (carbs), fats, and proteins.

Put simply, your blood sugar levels rise after eating. From there, your pancreas releases insulin, which moves the sugar into storage, saving it for when you need energy later. If you have type 1 diabetes, your pancreas is unable to make insulin, or not enough of it, causing your blood sugars to rise alarmingly high or fall dangerously low.

While some people are genetically predisposed to type 1 diabetes, it can also be triggered by the body attacking itself, known as an autoimmune reaction. While type 1 diabetes is usually seen in children or teens, there is a slim chance of adult onset.

Around 5–10 percent of people with diabetes have type 1. There is currently no cure for the condition, nor is there a known way to prevent it from developing.

TYPE 2 DIABETES

The biggest distinction between type 1 and type 2 diabetes is that you can prevent type 2 with a healthy lifestyle. About 90–95 percent of all people with diabetes have type 2, and it tends to arise in adulthood. However, over the last decade, more and more children are being diagnosed with type 2 diabetes due to poor diet and lack of exercise.

Lilian was only diagnosed because her blurry vision brought her to the doctor, but some people won't experience any symptoms. If you have any uncertainty, a simple blood sugar test will let you know. And if caught early, there is a chance of reversing type 2 diabetes with healthy food, weight loss, and staying active.

GESTATIONAL DIABETES

Some pregnant women are diagnosed with gestational diabetes when their bodies can no longer generate enough insulin. This tends to happen in the later stages of pregnancy. Overweight and obese women are more prone to gestational diabetes, as they may already have some insulin resistance.

After delivery, the condition goes away for most women with gestational diabetes. If a woman still experiences these symptoms after birth, it's then considered type 2 diabetes. Unfortunately, even when gestational diabetes goes away, 50 percent of all women who experienced gestational diabetes during pregnancy develop type 2 diabetes later in life.

What Increases Your Risk of Diabetes? ··································

If you have any of the following, you are considered at risk for developing type 2 diabetes:

- Have a family member with diabetes
- Are over forty-five years in age
- Exercise fewer than three times a week
- Had gestational diabetes
- Are overweight or obese
- Have prediabetes

Believe it or not, one third of all American adults have prediabetes. Over 80 percent of them don't even know it! What's the line between prediabetes and diabetes? It all comes down to blood sugar levels. In a prediabetic person, these levels are higher than those of a healthy person, but not as high as a person with diabetes.

Prediabetes on its own increases your risk of not only type 2 diabetes, but also stroke and heart disease. Thankfully, if you have prediabetes or type 2 diabetes, you can drastically reduce your symptoms, and even revert them altogether! How? It's all about lifestyle.

Eating for Diabetes

Getting Started ···

We always hear about eating healthier. It drones in the background of ads, pours out of doctors' mouths, and shouts at you from food packaging. And I bet when you think about healthy eating, you picture a bland, greens-heavy salad. The good news is that healthy foods don't have to be boring! Thanks to seasonings, dressings, and enhancing texture, your meals can be inspired and flavorful (more on that later).

If you've followed my cookbook journey, you probably know that I favor the Mediterranean diet. What's compelling is that *all* the diet-related suggestions for people with diabetes perfectly reflect the principles of the Mediterranean diet. It's all about incorporating foods that fuel you (think whole grains, healthy fats, fresh produce), while cutting down on foods that drain you (like sugary treats and heavily processed carbs).

Interestingly, the Mediterranean diet has one of the highest rates of adherence. What does this mean for you? Most people find sticking to this diet works well for their lifestyle, primarily because it is not about restriction but about identifying healthy, Mediterranean-esque alternatives.

A life pillar I've always believed is that Mediterranean cuisine is for everyone. Not only does the research support it, as I've discussed in my previous cookbooks, but so do my numerous clients. Even Lilian, after a year of abiding by the Mediterranean diet (and the recipes in this book!), has discovered newfound control over her life by reducing her diabetes symptoms. She's elevated her energy levels, stabilized her weight, and even reduced the numbing in her limbs! Research has shown that for people with prediabetes, sticking to a Mediterranean diet can reduce their odds of developing type 2 diabetes by a whopping 23 percent.

Since I began my career, I've tailored my Mediterranean-inspired recipes for just about every lifestyle: international athletes, newborns, stay-at-home moms, and many people with chronic illnesses. Why? Because the Mediterranean diet has life-changing benefits, from reducing heart disease to increasing longevity, and even promoting healthy aging.

While the name "Mediterranean diet" can be misleading, because it's more of a lifestyle, the principles align with overarching best practices for your health. Here is a quick guide that offers you insight into what food is favored with this lifestyle:

EAT LOTS OF	EAT MINDFULLY	EAT LESS
DAILY	1–2X A WEEK	1–3X A MONTH
Vegetables, legumes, whole grains, extra-virgin olive oil, fish, seafood, tofu, spices, herbs, fruits, nuts, and seeds	Chicken, turkey, eggs, cheese, and dairy products	Red meat, sugar-laden drinks, processed meat, deli meats, refined oils, refined carbs, and sugary treats

Low-Glycemic Index Foods

Most people with diabetes are aware of the glycemic index. The index is founded on the idea that not all carbs are equal. For example, someone getting 100 grams of carbs in a day from donuts, bagels, and soda is very different from someone getting their 100 grams of carbs from vegetables, quinoa, and tofu. By default, we mentally may group the former as "unhealthy" and the latter as "healthy," but why?

The ideology of not all carbs being equal stems from how carbs react in your body. To understand this better, we must acknowledge the different types of carbs, how they are categorized, and how they are broken down in your body:

TYPE OF CARB	CATEGORY	HOW IT'S PROCESSED
SUGARS Carbohydrates that can be added to any food, such as juice, soda, processed foods, packaged treats, and desserts	**SIMPLE CARBOHYDRATES** The most basic form of carbohydrates	They break down quickly in your digestive tract, releasing bursts of glucose, spiking your blood sugar levels
STARCHES Carbohydrates that deliver essential vitamins and minerals during digestion, including whole grains, potatoes, pasta, and corn	**COMPLEX CARBOHYDRATES** Simple sugars strung together in long, complex chains	Starches must be broken down into sugars before they're used for energy. This reduces blood sugar fluctuations
FIBER Indigestible carbohydrates that are usually found in the cells of plants, such as vegetables, beans, and berries		Your body cannot break down fiber, meaning it will not affect your blood sugar levels. It also keeps you feeling full for longer

Since the Mediterranean diet tends to prioritize low-glycemic index foods, you can see the similarities in the chart above with the one below. Keep in mind, none of the foods in the "Eat Less" category are foods to completely cut out. Simply consider how often you eat them, and whether or not there are better options available.

EAT LOTS OF	EAT MINDFULLY	EAT LESS
Foods that *do not* affect your blood sugar levels	Foods that *may* affect your blood sugar levels	Foods that *will* spike your blood sugar levels
Non-starchy vegetables, nuts, seeds, eggs, beans, extra-virgin olive oil, fish, avocados, soy, tofu, whole grains, and most fruits	Berries, plain yogurt, carrots, sweet potatoes, milk, cheese, butter, sweet corn, bananas, and multi-grain bread	Cakes, cookies, candy, sweetened yogurts, processed grains (white rice, white bread, etc.), fruit juice, sodas, and honey

The Diabetes Food Pyramid

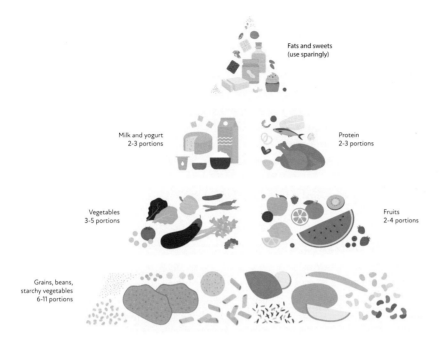

Fats and sweets
(use sparingly)

Milk and yogurt
2-3 portions

Protein
2-3 portions

Vegetables
3-5 portions

Fruits
2-4 portions

Grains, beans,
starchy vegetables
6-11 portions

Now that we've covered the basics of eating for diabetes and the relevance of a Mediterranean diet, I would like to introduce you to your new food pyramid, created by the American Diabetes Association! This may look similar to your typical food pyramid, but there are a few notable differences. The biggest change is that instead of grouping food by their classification (protein, diary, grain, etc.), they are grouped by their protein and carb content. This is why you'll see cheese in the "meat" group instead of dairy, because it has a higher protein content than other dairy products.

Grains and Starches (the Carbohydrates)

The base of your new food pyramid is composed of grains and starches. These grains include rice, pasta, bread, and cereal, while the starches include starchy vegetables, such as peas, corn, and potatoes, as well as a variety of beans. These two groups are combined because a slice of bread has roughly the same carb content as the starchy foods mentioned above.

Aim for **6–11 servings a day of grains and starches**. However, with diabetes, it is always safer to err on the side of caution and stick to the lower end of this range.

Vegetables

Vegetables are packed with essential nutrients, such as vitamins, minerals, and fiber. They are low in fats and make the perfect addition to "healthify" any meal. This group excludes the starchy vegetables mentioned above. For this group, prioritize broccoli, cabbage, lettuce, spinach, cauliflower, tomatoes, and cucumbers.

You need a minimum of **3–5 servings a day of vegetables**, but more will never hurt!

Fruits

Fruits make up their own category, as they hold more carbohydrates than vegetables, but not as much as grains and starches. This is why when referencing the glycemic index, most fruits end up in the "Eat Mindfully" category, as opposed to "Eat Lots of."

Oranges, berries, pears, apricots, pineapples, peaches, bananas, and more make up this piece of the pyramid.

Plan for **2–4 servings a day of fruits**, and try not to exceed the maximum.

Meat and Meat Substitutes

Higher up on the pyramid sits meats and meat substitutes, focusing on your protein intake. This group encompasses beef, turkey, chicken, eggs, fish, cheese, peanut butter, and tofu. While all meat is organized together, they are not all equal (as you saw in the above charts). Opt for leaner meats on a regular basis, such as fish, seafood, and tofu, and reserve the others for special occasions.

You need **4–6 servings a day of meat and meat substitutes**. Keep in mind, a serving of meat is usually around 1 ounce.

Milk Products

While milk does have protein, its protein content is less than meat and meat substitutes. As such, it has its own group on the diabetes food pyramid. Similar to meat, not all milk products are equal—try to prioritize those with less saturated fats.

Choose **2–3 servings a day of milk products**.

Sweets, Treats, and Alcohol

This group is high in fats and sugars and should be limited as much as possible. That does not mean cutting them out of your life, but be mindful of how often you're reaching for these convenient foods, such as chips, baked goods, fried foods, and prepackaged options.

Aim for **2–3 servings a <u>week</u> of sweet treats**!

Building Healthy Habits

Start Slow

Food is the most integral part of managing diabetes, as a proper diet reduces your risk of a multitude of health conditions, such as heart disease. However, the approach most people take is simply ineffective and unattainable. Think of all those ads showing people who have lost X amount of weight in one month. You probably don't realize that 90 percent of those individuals will gain all the weight back, and then some. This boomerang effect is extremely common; however, there are ways to prevent it!

First things first, never make more than one change at the same time. For example, try starting by reducing one serving of sweets a day. Once you feel confident and comfortable with this step, and don't feel the urge to binge, try adding an extra serving of greens to every meal. Whether that means snacking on edamame or adding cucumbers to your dinner is completely up to you and your preferences. Personally, I'm not a fan of raw spinach, so I always swap it out for kale.

Portion Control

Another aspect of diet is portions. The size of your portions can directly affect your insulin levels (more food means more sugar in the blood). As such, it's important you eat portions that leave you feeling comfortable and full—not hungry and not bloated. This will look different for everyone!

If you're not sure where to start, try dividing up your plate using the diabetes food pyramid. The first quarter will be grains and starches, the second quarter will be protein and dairy, and the final half vegetables and fruit.

Stay Consistent

As mentioned above, more food means a heightened blood sugar level, which can be dire to diabetics. This means that staying consistent with your meals and their timing is important. Ensure you're eating a full three meals a day, with no more than six hours between each. It's also integral to eat the same amount (at least the same amount of carbs) at every meal.

This may seem excessive, but if you wait too long between meals, your blood sugar level will drop too low. On the flip side, if you eat too much too quickly, your blood sugar level will spike too high. Both of these outcomes can result in disastrous effects, causing permanent damage to your body!

Meal Planning ···

In a similar vein, meal planning can help you stay consistent with your meals. Organizing ahead of time will save you money, effort, and unwanted blood sugar changes. If you're new to meal planning, feel free to start with my weekly guide below. This plan uses recipes straight from this cookbook and should give you a strong foundation, getting you comfortable with planning ahead. Feel free to swap the recipes for ones you're most interested in trying.

A few things to keep in mind when you're planning meals:

1. Check what's in your kitchen first, and use up what you have.
2. Build meals around similar Ingredients, ensuring everything gets used and to save money.
3. Avoid recipes with special Ingredients. (If you don't know where it is in your grocery store, skip it!)
4. Prioritize whatever produce is in season.
5. Consider frozen produce; it's just as nutritious as fresh.
6. Plan for and use your leftovers as lunches or dinners.
7. Cook in bulk to save time and energy.
8. Know what you enjoy eating and rotate in your favorite recipes.

SUNDAY	MONDAY	TUESDAY	WEDNESDAY	THURSDAY	FRIDAY	SATURDAY
Breakfast recipe #1 x 3	Breakfast recipe #1, leftovers	Breakfast recipe #1, leftovers	Breakfast recipe #2 (quick)	Breakfast recipe #3 (prepped overnight)	Breakfast recipe #3, leftovers	Breakfast recipe #4 (eggs or something with cooking)
Lunch recipe #1 x 2	Lunch recipe #1, leftovers	Dinner recipe #1, leftovers	Lunch recipe #2	Lunch recipe #2, leftovers	Dinner recipe #3, leftovers	Lunch recipe #3 (something that takes longer)
Dinner recipe #1 x 3	Dinner recipe #1, leftovers	Dinner recipe #2 x 2	Dinner recipe #2, leftovers	Dinner recipe #3 x 2	Dinner recipe #4 x 2	Dinner recipe #4, leftovers
		Prep lunch recipe #2 x 2 (quick, like a sandwich)	Prep breakfast recipe #3			

Healthy Carbs ··

I've had many clients with diabetes who thought they had to avoid carbs. I'm here to clear the air and inform you that you can have carbs. As the glycemic index shows, it just matters which kinds of carbs you're choosing.

I'll bet when you hear "carbs," your mind goes to sugary treats and processed bread. And while those certainly are laden with carbs, so are legumes, quinoa, and even grapefruit! The latter carbs are not just better for you because they are on the lower end of the glycemic index, they also keep you fuller for longer, which prevents cravings and binging.

Favoring these carbs over convenient and processed options prevents your blood sugar from spiking, while also protecting you from heart disease, stroke, and some cancers.

Healthy Fats ··

Like carbs, some fats are better for us than others.

Saturated fats typically come from animal-derived products, such as red meats and dairy. However, they can also be found in prepackaged and fried foods. Saturated fats increase your level of "bad" cholesterol, called LDL.

Trans fats are primarily found in fast and processed foods. Trans fat doesn't just increase "bad" cholesterol levels, it also decreases healthy cholesterol, known as HDL. Unfortunately, this kind of fat is commonly disguised on Ingredient lists as "shortening" or "partially hydrogenated oil."

Both saturated and trans fats are found in a wide variety of our foods, which is why it's important to identify them and search for "healthy" fat alternatives!

So what is "healthy" fat? Monounsaturated and polyunsaturated fats are considered heart healthy because they lower your LDL levels, which in turn lowers your risk of heart disease. Some healthy fats include avocado, nuts, extra-virgin olive oil, nut butters, and fish—which just so happen to land on the lower end of the glycemic index!

If you tend to favor foods with saturated and trans fats (I'm looking at all you butter fiends), there's no need to worry! I've put together a chart below that offers healthy fat alternatives for your go-tos.

HIGH "UNHEALTHY" FAT FOODS	HIGH "HEALTHY" FAT ALTERNATIVES
Butter, shortening, hydrogenated oils	Extra-virgin olive oil, vegetable oil
Ground meat, red meat, sausages	Turkey, white-meat chicken, fish
Ice cream	Sorbet, sherbet, frozen yogurt
Cookies, pies, cakes	Low-sugar puddings, wafer cookies
Fried foods	Grilled, roasted, steamed, boiled foods
Chips	Nuts and seeds
2% milk, cream	Soy milk, oat milk, almond milk
Premade spreads	Nut butters, homemade jams

Watch What You Drink

We've all heard, "Drink more water!" And it's certainly a helpful guideline, but people with diabetes should listen a tad closer. When you're dehydrated, the water stores in your body become depleted, resulting in a higher concentration of sugar in your blood. To prevent this spike, make water part of your daily routine. Personally, I own one of those huge water bottles with the time markers. It's an easy way to track my intake.

While water should be your default drink, you don't have to always rely on water straight from the tap. Spice it up with fruit and herbal infusions! I love rosemary and lemon or blueberries with thyme. Because water is sugar-free, it won't cause any changes to your blood sugar, and it's also calorie-free.

Pop/soda, juice, and alcoholic beverages can all affect your blood sugar levels. And while I never recommend cutting something completely out of your diet, I do suggest keeping these options to a minimum.

Amping Up Your Dishes

I'm going to let you in on a few of my go-to Mediterranean secrets that elevate any dish from "meh" to "I could eat this every day!" These are tips and tricks I picked up during my culinary training around the Mediterranean Sea, and they have empowered my clients to enjoy foods they once found boring.

1. Experiment with Acids

Our go-to for seasoning tends to be salt and pepper. And while tried and true, they often lack the jazz you're looking for. In addition to reaching for those bottles, consider some acids. I suggest experimenting with citrus, such as lemon juice, or vinegars. Add them to your sauces, stews, and salads to brighten up the entire meal!

2. Timing Is Everything

The default seems to be seasoning foods before cooking them. The issue with this is that you're literally cooking off the flavor of your seasonings. Obviously, it all comes down to how strong you want your seasonings to be, but if you prefer a commanding flavor profile, season after the heat. However, if you're more into softer flavors, season before the heat! Timing really is everything when it comes to your seasonings.

3. Fresh Herbs

I love spending my weekends exploring the neighborhood farmer's market. Not only is it my favorite spot for fresh produce, I also swear by their herb selection. Similar to seasonings, different herbs must be introduced to your dish at different times. Hearty herbs, including sage, marjoram, and rosemary, should be added early on in the cooking process so they have time to release and maximize their flavor. On the flip side, delicate herbs such as chives, basil, and parsley should be added at the last minute because they wilt and don't hold onto their flavor as well. This is why these herbs tend to be used as garnish.

4. Add Umami

Umami means "essence of deliciousness" in Japanese. And who doesn't want that? Most people describe umami as meaty and complex. An easy way you can incorporate umami into your dishes is with a few common kitchen staples. Worcestershire sauce, soy sauce, aged cheese, kimchi, and mushrooms all represent the umami flavor and are easy additives to any meal.

5. Multiple Textures

Remember earlier when I said healthy food directs your mind straight to bland salads? The main reason people detest salads is because of their lack of texture! Chewing leaf after leaf sounds awful, which is why people have given salads a bad reputation. But what if you could eat salads without any leaves? It all comes down to texture.

I never make a meal without all three forms of texture: creamy, crunchy/crispy, and chewy. Next time you're tossing a salad, swap out bland Ingredients for legumes (chewy), nuts or seeds (crunchy), and avocado (creamy). Finish off by topping with a variety of vegetables and a delicious sauce. Push yourself and try incorporating all three textures into every one of your meals!

Lifestyle Changes

Dietary changes certainly make a meaningful impact on your diabetes symptoms, but it doesn't end there. As with the Mediterranean diet, food alone only makes up part of the lifestyle. If you immerse yourself in all aspects of this lifestyle, you won't just feel better, you will feel in control of your symptoms.

Find Movement You Love

Like salads, we have a preconceived picture of exercise: painful, intense, and unpleasant. And I'll be honest, there are certain exercises that will feel like that for you. For me, it's running! Thankfully—for all of us—there are more forms of movement than you can count.

I cannot stress this point enough: find movement you love. This will completely transform the way you approach exercise. It will no longer feel agonizing, but uplifting. I have some clients who have fallen in love with Pilates (low impact), swimming (reduced joint pain), hiking (sightseeing), and weight lifting (muscle building).

You may be wondering, how do I find movement I actually enjoy? Well, it all comes down to what your body can handle, what your mind wants, and what results you're looking for. Here are some tips to help you out:

1. Try New Things

Sign up for new classes, experimenting with a variety of techniques and motions. Most gyms offer class passes, which allow you to jump between different class selections, giving you a chance to find a few you like. Into dancing? Try barre or Zumba classes. Into loud, high-energy music? Sign up for spin or kickboxing classes. Want comradery? Opt for bootcamp or Pilates. Need to start slow? Jump into a yoga flow!

If you don't live near any gyms or just aren't comfortable with them, you can find workout videos on YouTube. There are so many options out there, but I really enjoy them when I'm in a time crunch and still want to get a sweat in.

2. Make the Time

I know, I know, we've all been there. "I just don't have the time" is a common phrase for everyone. But when you're committed to a lifestyle change, it's important to pencil in time for exercise. Find time slots that work for you and stick to them. Simply, add movement into your schedule so you have something to hold yourself accountable.

I prefer my workouts when I'm done with all my daily chores, which is usually after work in the early evening. However, I have friends who set their alarms thirty minutes early to fit their movement into their mornings. I've tried exercising at all times of the day and decided that after 5:00 p.m. works best for me and my needs. What works for you?

3. Convenience Is Key

This tip differs depending on the exercise you decide on, but these are some tricks I've picked up that motivate me to get moving: laying out my workout clothes the night before, using YouTube videos when I'm stuck at home, selecting my routine before my scheduled workout time, paying for a membership with a gym nearby, and getting protein and water ready before I get going. Keeping things as convenient as possible prevents excuses and allows you to dive headfirst into your workout.

4. Changes Take Time

You will not see visible changes from your workouts for the first three months. Some people won't see anything for longer. *This is normal.* If your goal is to gain muscle, lose weight, or get toned, I always suggest measuring yourself and noting it down. Once a month, measure the same places again and see if there's any change. I didn't notice my own muscle growth until I compared my measurements! When you see yourself every day, it's difficult to discern any differences. Be patient and trust the process. The more you believe this is a lifestyle, the more likely you'll exercise out of enjoyment, pushing the progress aside.

5. Grab a Buddy

I can promise you, you're not the only person in your social circle looking to improve your fitness. Grab a friend or family member and keep each other accountable. Better yet, find a group of people and make your exercise a movement party! There's no reason workouts have to be boring or solo. If you're social, this is the perfect excuse to recruit a buddy.

Movement is especially important for overweight people with diabetes. This is because when an individual has excess weight, their body becomes less sensitive to insulin. In fact, there are some studies that find fat cells are much more resistant to insulin than muscle cells. People with diabetes who incorporate movement into their lifestyle appear to reduce excess sugar in the bloodstream. In turn, this prevents the body from creating extra insulin, while keeping sugar out of fat cells.

Find a Sleep Routine ·····························

There are a variety of factors that affect sleep for people with diabetes. In fact, 50 percent of people with type 2 diabetes report sleep issues caused by their unstable blood sugar levels.

If you eat right before bed, or indulge in a sugary treat in the evening, it can lead to high blood sugar levels during sleep. When this happens, your kidneys overcompensate by forcing you awake for frequent bathroom trips. Hello, disturbed sleep! High blood sugar levels can also cause tiredness, headaches, and a pervasive thirstiness, all of which interfere with sleep quality. On the flip side, if you go without eating much at all in the evening, you're likely to experience low blood sugar levels during sleep. This increase can trigger night sweats, nightmares, or anger and confusion upon waking.

As you can see, good quality sleep is a common concern for people with diabetes. I always suggest reaching out to your doctor if you experience poor sleep. However, there are some things in your control to help prevent sleeplessness:

- Keep your blood sugar regulated with a healthy diet (use recipes in this cookbook!).
- Be consistent with your wake up and lights out times.
- Make your bedroom cool, dark, and quiet.
- Ensure your mattress and pillows are comfy.
- Move daily to release extra energy.
- Remove electronics from your bedroom (including your phone).
- Stop drinking beverages one hour before your bedtime.

Cut Down Stress

As a whole, our society is far too stressed out. This is due to a combination of factors, such as social media, invasive technology, societal pressures, work, and of course, the people around us. It may feel like a losing battle to cut down stress, but there are reasons it's even more important for people with diabetes.

According to the Cleveland Clinic, cortisol, known as the stress hormone, has an enormous impact on your blood sugar levels. When you experience an increase in cortisol from a stressful event, it counteracts the effects of insulin, causing insulin resistance. Since controlling blood sugar levels is integral to diabetes, reducing stress as much as possible can ease your symptoms.

Stress can also lead to binging as a form of coping. In these cases, people reach for whatever is available and convenient, which tends to land on the higher end of the glycemic index, leading to an unwanted spike in blood sugar levels.

Reducing stress isn't just advantageous for diabetes but for your overall health. Chronic stress can lead to a multitude of health conditions, including digestive problems, heart disease, heightened blood pressure, poor concentration, insomnia, headaches, and muscle pain. To keep yourself calm during stressful situations, find what works for you. I love putting on a meditation app when I feel overwhelmed. However, there's an array of options, such as yoga, walks in nature, journaling, exercise, reaching out to loved ones, and finding a creative outlet.

Create a Support System

While you make these changes to your lifestyle, lean on your close ones for support. Sometimes support looks like allowing you to rant, offering you advice, or even holding you through a good cry. This may seem like an obvious lifestyle suggestion, but not everyone has a supportive family or an extensive friend group. I know when I moved to a new city with my immediate family, it took us almost a year to form close-knit buddies.

If you're in need of a support system and aren't sure where to start, I recommend joining a club (or a fitness class!), signing up for volunteering, researching festivals and events in your area, or participating in online forums. I've even made friends by visiting my local library. Remember, people who want to get to know you will ask questions and be engaged in what you say. It's also important you put yourself out there by reciprocating those cues.

Create a Professional Care Team ····························

Doctor visits can be stressful—so stressful we avoid them altogether. But one thing I've learned as a life coach is that the longer you wait, the worse the news becomes. It's vital to prioritize these checkups. Usually at the time of diagnosis, your doctor will recommend a set number of annual visits. I advise that you stick to that number, and if anything unusual pops up between, schedule an additional appointment. Your health is the essence of who you are. Do not push it aside because of discomfort. At the end of the day, discomfort is a sign of growth.

On top of visits with your family doctor, I always recommend that my clients with diabetes enlist the support of a diabetes educator, a registered dietitian, an endocrinologist, and an optometrist. I understand not everyone has access to these professionals through their health care system. If that's the case, look for online forums that fact-check their sources.

Cut Out Smoking ····································

Similar to drinking alcohol, the pros of smoking cigarettes simply do not outweigh the cons. When you smoke, your body's cells become inflamed, which blocks your cells from responding and accepting the insulin, leaving an excess of insulin in your blood. Interestingly, people who smoke are 30–40 percent more likely to acquire type 2 diabetes. And if you already have diabetes, smoking can cause trouble with your insulin dosing.

The good news is, no matter how long you've been a smoker, within twenty minutes of quitting you'll start reaping the benefits. When you do quit, you'll have to check your blood sugar levels more often because they will probably go down, as your cells will start accepting the insulin into them again. If you use nicotine patches (which is totally acceptable), they will increase insulin levels, as smoking does, so keep that in mind as well.

Dive into the Recipes ····································

Now that we've covered eating for and living with diabetes, I hope you're ready to invest in yourself and your new lifestyle by diving into these recipes. Remember, starting slowly is key, so whether you want to begin by adding a few new recipes a week or adding more movement, pick what feels the most realistic to you.

I'm excited for this new phase in your life. As with all my clients, I'd like to remind you that you're not alone! These changes may feel intimidating, but your reading this far proves that you're prepared for the challenge. Diabetes is without a doubt a difficult condition to navigate, but with the tools we've discussed, I'm positive that like Lilian, you'll experience a newfound control over your symptoms.

I wish you and your family delicious dinners, mindful movement, and plenty of laughter.

X
Veronica Miles

Allergen Legend

DAIRY FREE
DF

NUT FREE
NF

EGG FREE
EF

SUGAR FREE
SF

GLUTEN FREE
GF

VEGETARIAN
VE

VEGAN

VG

Bibliography/Notes

Cai, Cindy Xinji. "Diabetes and Your Eyes." Johns Hopkins Medicine, December 22, 2022. https://www.hopkinsmedicine.org/health/conditions-and-diseases/diabetes-and-your-eyes-what-you-need-to-know.

Centers for Disease Control and Prevention. "Gestational Diabetes and Pregnancy." July 14, 2022. https://www.cdc.gov/pregnancy/diabetes-gestational.html.

Centers for Disease Control and Prevention. "Prediabetes." December 30, 2022. https://www.cdc.gov/diabetes/basics/prediabetes.html.

Centers for Disease Control and Prevention. "Smoking and Diabetes." May 5, 2022. https://www.cdc.gov/tobacco/campaign/tips/diseases/diabetes.html.

Centers for Disease Control and Prevention. "What Is Diabetes?" April 24, 2023. https://www.cdc.gov/diabetes/basics/diabetes.html.

Cleveland Clinic. "Insulin Resistance." December 16, 2021. https://my.clevelandclinic.org/health/diseases/22206-insulin-resistance.

Esposito, Katherine, Maria Ida Maiorino, Giuseppe Bellastella, Paolo Chiodini, Demosthenes Panagiotakos, and Dario Giugliano. "A Journey into a Mediterranean Diet and Type 2 Diabetes: A Systematic Review with Meta-analysis." U.S. National Library of Medicine, August 10, 2015. https://pubmed.ncbi.nlm.nih.gov/26260349/.

Harvard T.H. Chan School of Public Health. "Diet Review: Mediterranean Diet." The Nutrition Source, April 19, 2023. https://www.hsph.harvard.edu/nutritionsource/healthy-weight/diet-reviews/mediterranean-diet/.

National Institute of Diabetes and Digestive and Kidney Diseases. "Diabetes Statistics," February 2023. https://www.niddk.nih.gov/health-information/health-statistics/diabetes-statistics.

Obesity Action Coalition. "Understanding Excess Weight and Its Role in Type 2 Diabetes." Honor Health, 2011. https://www.honorhealth.com/medical-services/bariatric-weight-loss-surgery/patient-education-and-support/comorbidities-type-2-diabetes.

Quinn, Laurie, Bingqian Zhu, Mary C. Kapella , Ulf G. Bronas, Eileen G. Collins, Chang G. Park, Laurie Ruggiero, and Cynthia Fritschi. "Relationship between Sleep Disturbance and Self-care in Adults with Type 2 Diabetes." U.S. National Library of Medicine, September 2018. https://pubmed.ncbi.nlm.nih.gov/29931420/.

Runge, Marschall S. "Weighing the Facts: The Tough Truth about Weight Loss." Michigan Medicine. University of Michigan, April 12, 2017. https://www.michiganmedicine.org/health-lab/weighing-facts-tough-truth-about-weight-loss.

BREAKFAST

Mediterranean Frittata

Prep time: 5 minutes
Cook time: 20 minutes
Total time: 25 minutes

LEVEL 3: MODERATE

. . . .

Swap out your regular omelets for this Mediterranean Frittata. Packed with briny feta, juicy cherry tomatoes, and fresh chives, it's perfectly seasoned and bakes in less than 15 minutes! Loaded with protein and linked to reduced heart disease and increased eye health, eggs are a reliable Ingredient for your busy mornings.

. . . .

MAKES 2 SERVINGS

6 large **eggs**
¼ cup chopped **chives**
Handful of fresh **basil**
2 tablespoons **heavy cream**
1 teaspoon **Italian seasoning**
½ teaspoon **Himalayan salt**
½ teaspoon ground **black pepper**
½ cup crumbled **feta cheese,**
   divided
1 tablespoon **extra-virgin olive oil**
½ **bell pepper,** chopped
½ cup halved **cherry tomatoes,**
   divided

1. Preheat the oven to 400°F.

2. Whisk the eggs, chives, basil, heavy cream, Italian seasoning, salt, and pepper together in a large bowl until well combined. Whisk in 6 tablespoons of the feta and set aside.

3. Heat the olive oil in a 9-inch oven-safe skillet over medium-high heat. Add the bell peppers and sauté for 4–5 minutes until they soften. Stir in ¼ cup of the cherry tomatoes and cook for an additional 1–2 minutes, until tender.

4. Add the sautéed bell peppers and tomatoes to the egg mixture and stir with a spatula to distribute the vegetables, then add the remaining 2 tablespoons of feta and ¼ cup of cherry tomatoes. Mix to combine.

5. Pour the batter into the oven-safe skillet and return to medium-high heat for 1 minute, until the perimeter is slightly golden. Transfer the skillet to the oven and bake for 10–15 minutes, until the eggs are set.

6. Remove from the oven and transfer to a wire rack to cool. Divide between two plates and serve.

NUTRITION	Per Serving	% of Daily Value
Calories	350	
Total Fat	25 g	32%
Saturated Fat	10.7 g	54%
Polyunsaturated Fat	3.2 g	—
Monounsaturated Fat	8.9 g	—
Trans Fat	—	—
Cholesterol	420 mg	140%
Sodium	370 mg	16%
Total Carbohydrates	6 g	2%
Dietary Fiber	1 g	3%
Total Sugars	3 g	—
Protein	25 g	50%
Vitamin A	466 mcg	50%
Vitamin C	33.6 mg	35%
Vitamin D	3.3 mcg	15%
Potassium	395 mg	8%
Calcium	292 mg	20%
Iron	3.2 mg	20%

Cinnamon Roll Porridge with Cranberries

Prep time: 5 minutes
Cook time: 5 minutes
Total time: 10 minutes

LEVEL 2: EASY

. . . .

Imagine biting into a fresh, crisp French pastry as part of your morning routine. Thanks to this recipe, you don't have to dream it up—you can experience all the flavors of a fruit-studded cinnamon roll in a quick, healthy oatmeal porridge! Rich cinnamon, syrupy honey, and tart cranberries come together to create a delicious and nutritious breakfast.

. . . .

MAKES 1 SERVING

1 cup nondairy **milk**
½ cup gluten-free **quick oats**
1 **banana**, mashed,
    plus ¼ banana, sliced
1 teaspoon ground **cardamom**
1 teaspoon **raw honey**
¼ cup dried **cranberries**
1 teaspoon ground **cinnamon**
2 tablespoons **almond butter**

1. Combine the milk, oats, mashed banana, cardamom, and honey in a small saucepan over medium-high heat. Cook for 5 minutes, stirring occasionally, until it thickens.

2. Transfer to a small heat-safe bowl, add the cranberries and cinnamon, and stir until well combined.

3. Top with the almond butter and banana slices. Serve immediately or refrigerate for the next day and serve cold.

NUTRITION	Per Serving	% of Daily Value
Calories	310	—
Total Fat	11 g	14%
Saturated Fat	4.4 g	22%
Polyunsaturated Fat	1.9 g	—
Monounsaturated Fat	3.5 g	—
Trans Fat	—	—
Cholesterol	20 mg	7%
Sodium	90 mg	4%
Total Carbohydrates	56 g	20%
Dietary Fiber	10 g	36%
Total Sugars	12 g	—
Protein	15 g	30%
Vitamin A	109 mcg	10%
Vitamin C	5 mg	6%
Vitamin D	0.1 mcg	—
Potassium	701 mg	15%
Calcium	296 mg	25%
Iron	—	—

Zucchini, Pea, and Halloumi Fritters

Prep time: 10 minutes
Cook time: 15 minutes
Total time: 25 minutes

LEVEL 3: MODERATE

. . . .

Traditionally made from a mixture of sheep and goat milk, Halloumi dates back to 1191. Loaded with protein and calcium, this salty cheese elevates any recipe—including these fritters. Thanks to the zucchini, this dish may improve digestion, strengthen eyesight, and aid weight loss!

. . . .

MAKES 10 PANCAKES

3 medium **zucchinis**, grated
1 cup coarsely grated **Halloumi**
1 cup **almond flour**
½ cup frozen **peas**
¼ cup chopped fresh **dill** or **mint**
2 **eggs**, lightly beaten
1½ teaspoons **Himalayan salt**
½ teaspoon ground **black pepper**
3 tablespoons **extra-virgin olive oil**

1. Combine the zucchini, Halloumi, almond flour, peas, dill or mint, eggs, salt, and black pepper in a medium bowl and mix well.

2. Place the olive oil in a large frying pan over medium-high heat.

3. Spoon about 3 tablespoons of the batter per pancake into the frying pan and flatten slightly using a spatula.

4. Cook the pancakes for 3–4 minutes each, until golden, flipping halfway through. Place them onto paper towels to drain.

5. Repeat steps 3–4 until all the batter has been used.

6. Serve warm. Refrigerate leftovers in an airtight container for up to 3 days.

NUTRITION	Per Serving	% of Daily Value
Calories	60	—
Total Fat	4.5 g	6%
Saturated Fat	1.8 g	9%
Polyunsaturated Fat	0.3 g	—
Monounsaturated Fat	1.7 g	—
Trans Fat	—	—
Cholesterol	15 mg	5%
Sodium	85 mg	4%
Total Carbohydrates	2 g	1%
Dietary Fiber	—	—
Total Sugars	—	—
Protein	4 g	8%
Vitamin A	47.7 mcg	6%
Vitamin C	2.5 mg	2%
Vitamin D	0.2 mcg	—
Potassium	50 mg	2%
Calcium	92 mg	8%
Iron	0.4 mg	2%

Golden Shrimp and Avocado Toast

Prep time: 25 minutes
Cook time: 5 minutes
Total time: 30 minutes

LEVEL 3: MODERATE

. . . .

Seafood has been fundamental to Mediterranean cuisine since its creation. This recipe encompasses a fan favorite— juicy shrimp. Toss it with lime juice and paprika and layer it with fresh avocado slices, and you'll wonder why you didn't experiment with shrimp for breakfast before!

. . . .

MAKES 4 SERVINGS

1 pound shrimp, raw

Juice of 2 limes, divided

1 teaspoon smoked paprika

½ teaspoon kosher salt

¼ teaspoon cayenne pepper

4 slices whole-wheat bread, toasted

4 large avocados, sliced

½ large tomato, chopped

¼ cup chopped fresh cilantro, optional

1. Combine the shrimp, juice of 1 lime, smoked paprika, salt, and cayenne pepper in a medium bowl, tossing to combine. Cover the bowl with a dish towel or plastic wrap and refrigerate for 15–20 minutes to marinate.

2. Turn your grill to high. Arrange the shrimp on the grill and cook for 3–4 minutes, until golden.

3. Place the toast slices on a platter, then arrange the avocado slices on the toast. Top with the shrimp and garnish with the remaining lime juice, the tomatoes, and the cilantro, if desired. Serve warm.

NUTRITION	Per Serving	% of Daily Value
Calories	470	—
Total Fat	30 g	38%
Saturated Fat	4.4 g	22%
Polyunsaturated Fat	4 g	—
Monounsaturated Fat	19.8 g	—
Trans Fat	—	—
Cholesterol	135 mg	45%
Sodium	115 mg	5%
Total Carbohydrates	28 g	10%
Dietary Fiber	15 g	54%
Total Sugars	2 g	—
Protein	29 g	58%
Vitamin A	273 mcg	30%
Vitamin C	31.1 mg	35%
Vitamin D	—	—
Potassium	1406 mg	30%
Calcium	108 mg	8%
Iron	2.4 mg	15%

Spinach Fritters

Prep time: 5 minutes
Cook time: 25 minutes
Total time: 30 minutes

LEVEL 4: CHALLENGING

. . . .

As a recipe and lifestyle coach, I love fiber, since it can aid weight loss, keep you satisfied, and control your blood sugar levels. Thankfully, both potatoes and spinach are treasure troves of fiber. If you have any leftover veggies lying around, this recipe is the perfect way to put them to use.

. . . .

MAKES 6 SERVINGS

1 tablespoon + 2 teaspoons extra-
    virgin olive oil, divided
1 cup diced potatoes
1 medium onion, diced
1 garlic clove, minced
½ cup spinach leaves
1⅓ cups chickpea flour
2 large eggs, lightly beaten
½ cup water
½ teaspoon salt

1. Heat 1 tablespoon of olive oil in a nonstick frying pan over medium-high heat. Stir in the diced potatoes and cook for 10 minutes, until they are lightly golden and start to soften.

2. Add the onion, garlic, and remaining 2 teaspoons of olive oil. Cook for another 5 minutes, stirring occasionally, until the onions soften.

3. Add the spinach and cook for 2 minutes, until the spinach wilts.

4. Whisk together the chickpea flour, eggs, water, and salt in a medium bowl. Pour the mixture into the pan and mix well, until the potatoes are coated with the mixture.

5. Decrease the heat to medium-low and cook for 5–7 minutes, until golden. Flip and cook for another 5 minutes, until golden. Remove from the heat.

6. Serve and enjoy! Refrigerate leftovers in an airtight container for up to 3 days.

NUTRITION	Per Serving	% of Daily Value
Calories	45	—
Total Fat	1.5 g	2%
Saturated Fat	0.2 g	1%
Polyunsaturated Fat	0.1 g	—
Monounsaturated Fat	1.1 g	—
Trans Fat	—	—
Cholesterol	—	—
Sodium	5 mg	—
Total Carbohydrates	7 g	3%
Dietary Fiber	1 g	4%
Total Sugars	1 g	—
Protein	1 g	2%
Vitamin A	141 mcg	15%
Vitamin C	7.8 mg	8%
Vitamin D	—	—
Potassium	165 mg	4%
Calcium	17 mg	2%
Iron	0.5 mg	2%

Pesto and Avocado Poached Eggs on Toast

Prep time: 10 minutes
Cook time: 10 minutes
Total time: 20 minutes

LEVEL 3: MODERATE

. . . .

Avocado toast has been a winning combination for years! Uplifted by fresh pesto, peppery parsley, and savory eggs, this recipe is part of our weekly repertoire at home. If you're new to poaching eggs, the secret is to keep the water swirling the entire time.

. . . .

MAKES 2 SERVINGS

2 slices whole-wheat bread, toasted
¼ cup pesto
1 avocado, sliced
2 tablespoons white vinegar
1¼ teaspoons salt, divided
2 medium eggs
½ medium red pepper, finely diced
¼ teaspoon ground black pepper
10 parsley leaves, finely chopped

1. Arrange the toast slices on a platter and spread a generous amount of pesto over each slice.

2. Place the avocado slices on top of the pesto.

3. Fill a large saucepan with water and bring to a boil over medium-high heat.

4. Reduce the heat to low and keep the water at a gentle boil. Add the white vinegar and 1 teaspoon of salt to the water.

5. Stir the water in a circular motion to create a vortex at the center of the pot. Carefully crack one egg into the center and keep stirring to maintain the water's vortex while the egg cooks. Adjust the heat, if needed, to maintain the gentle boil. Cook for 3½ minutes, until the egg white is firm and the yolk is loose.

6. Carefully scoop the poached egg out of the water and place it on top of one slice of avocado toast.

7. Repeat steps 5 and 6 for the remaining egg.

8. Top the poached eggs with diced red pepper and sprinkle them with black pepper, the remaining ¼ teaspoon of salt, and parsley. Serve warm and enjoy!

NUTRITION	Per Serving	% of Daily Value
Calories	582	—
Total Fat	34.1 g	44%
Saturated Fat	6.4 g	32%
Polyunsaturated Fat	5.1 g	—
Monounsaturated Fat	19.5 g	—
Trans Fat	—	—
Cholesterol	128 mg	43%
Sodium	985 mg	43%
Total Carbohydrates	31.4 g	11%
Dietary Fiber	11.4 g	39%
Total Sugars	5.1 g	—
Protein	16.2 g	32%
Vitamin A	979 mcg	110%
Vitamin C	75.6 mcg	80%
Vitamin D	0.9 mcg	4%
Potassium	875 mg	20%
Calcium	169 mg	15%
Iron	4.2 mg	25%

Simple Cheese and Veggie Omelet

Prep time: 5 minutes
Cook time: 5 minutes
Total time: 10 minutes

LEVEL 3: MODERATE

. . . .

If you're a gardener, try swapping in some of your fresh harvests for the fillings suggested here. And if you use locally sourced eggs, you'll dramatically reduce your meal's carbon footprint—in true Mediterranean fashion! What makes this omelet unique is the dynamic seasonings, including allspice, mint, and Spanish paprika.

. . . .

MAKES 2 SERVINGS

4 large eggs
2 tablespoons almond milk
1 teaspoon Himalayan salt
½ teaspoon ground black pepper
½ teaspoon Spanish paprika
¼ teaspoon ground allspice
¼ teaspoon baking powder
1½ teaspoons extra-virgin olive oil
3 tablespoons chopped fresh
   parsley
3 tablespoons chopped fresh mint

Optional fillings
½ cup halved cherry tomatoes
2 tablespoons sliced and pitted
   kalamata olives
¼–⅓ cup drained and quartered
   marinated artichoke hearts
2–4 tablespoons crumbled feta
   cheese, as desired

1. Whisk together the eggs, almond milk, salt, pepper, paprika, allspice, and baking powder in a medium bowl.

2. Heat the olive oil in a 10-inch skillet over medium-high heat. Tilt the skillet so the oil fully coats the bottom.

3. Pour the egg mixture into the skillet and stir it quickly with a spatula for 5 seconds. Push the cooked bits of the egg toward the center of the pan while tilting the pan to allow the raw egg to fill the empty spaces.

4. Cook the omelet for 1–2 minutes, until the bottom is golden and the eggs are nearly set, then remove from the heat. Add the toppings of your choice to one side of the omelet and fold over the empty side onto the toppings.

5. Slice the omelet in half, place each half on a serving plate, and sprinkle with parsley and mint, if desired.

NUTRITION	Per Serving	% of Daily Value
Calories	180	—
Total Fat	10 g	13%
Saturated Fat	3.2 g	16%
Polyunsaturated Fat	2.1 g	—
Monounsaturated Fat	3.4 g	—
Trans Fat	—	—
Cholesterol	170 mg	57%
Sodium	125 mg	5%
Total Carbohydrates	8 g	3%
Dietary Fiber	2 g	7%
Total Sugars	2 g	—
Protein	15 g	30%
Vitamin A	690 mcg	80%
Vitamin C	70.8 mg	80%
Vitamin D	2.2 mcg	10%
Potassium	393 mg	8%
Calcium	140 mg	10%
Iron	2.9 mg	15%

Raspberry and Granola Greek Yogurt

Prep time: 5 minutes
Cook time: 0 minutes
Total time: 1 hour 5 minutes

LEVEL 1: VERY EASY

. . . .

Everyone should start their feeding period with this probiotic-rich recipe. Why? Because the protein from the Greek yogurt keeps you energized and satisfied. Not only that, Greek yogurt also helps you maintain a healthy gut, while decreasing blood pressure. Now, this breakfast is a powerful start to the day!

. . . .

MAKES 1 SERVING

½ cup sugar-free, gluten-free granola
¼ cup fresh raspberries
1 teaspoon chia seeds
1 teaspoon roasted pumpkin seeds
1 teaspoon toasted sesame seeds
⅔ cup plain Greek yogurt
1 tablespoon maple syrup
½ teaspoon ground cinnamon

1. In an 8-ounce container, combine the granola, raspberries, chia seeds, pumpkin seeds, sesame seeds, Greek yogurt, and maple syrup.

2. Sprinkle the ground cinnamon on top of the granola-yogurt mixture.

3. Cover and refrigerate for 1 hour to chill, then serve.

NUTRITION	Per Serving	% of Daily Value
Calories	350	—
Total Fat	10 g	13%
Saturated Fat	1.4 g	7%
Polyunsaturated Fat	5.4 g	—
Monounsaturated Fat	2.4 g	—
Trans Fat	0.015 g	—
Cholesterol	10 mg	3%
Sodium	150 mg	7%
Total Carbohydrates	44 g	16%
Dietary Fiber	6 g	21%
Total Sugars	27 g	—
Protein	22 g	44%
Vitamin A	7.1 mcg	2%
Vitamin C	42 mg	10%
Vitamin D	—	—
Potassium	463 mg	10%
Calcium	262 mg	20%
Iron	1.8 mg	10%

Tunisian Shakshuka

Prep time: 10 minutes
Cook time: 20 minutes
Total time: 30 minutes

LEVEL 3: MODERATE

. . . .

Shakshuka is a popular Middle Eastern breakfast that originated in the Ottoman Empire. The combination of simmering tomatoes, poached eggs, and spicy harissa make for a nourishing and filling dish. Packed with important nutrients like vitamins B$_{12}$ and D, protein, and lycopene, this recipe will become a constant in your family rotation. If you can't find harissa, you can swap in any chili paste, add ⅓ teaspoon coriander seeds, and squeeze a lemon wedge when seasoning.

. . . .

MAKES 4 SERVINGS

2 tablespoons extra-virgin olive oil
1 onion, minced
2 red bell peppers, diced
2 garlic cloves, chopped
1 (15-ounce) can diced tomatoes
1 teaspoon spicy harissa
1 teaspoon salt
1 teaspoon black pepper
4 medium eggs
1 tablespoon chopped parsley

1. Heat the olive oil in a heavy cast-iron skillet over medium heat.

2. Add the onion and bell peppers and cook, stirring occasionally, until soft, about 5 minutes.

3. Stir in the garlic and cook for 1 minute. Stir in the tomatoes and harissa and cook, stirring, for 7 minutes.

4. Season with salt and pepper and add more harissa, if desired.

5. Make 4 holes in the tomato mixture with the back of a wooden spoon and crack an egg into each hole.

6. Cover the skillet and cook for 3–4 minutes, until the egg whites firm.

7. Sprinkle with fresh parsley and serve with pita or crusty bread, if desired.

NUTRITION	Per Serving	% of Daily Value
Calories	210	—
Total Fat	12 g	15%
Saturated Fat	2.3 g	12%
Polyunsaturated Fat	1.2 g	—
Monounsaturated Fat	4.6 g	—
Trans Fat	0.02 g	—
Cholesterol	165 mg	55%
Sodium	250 mg	11%
Total Carbohydrates	20 g	7%
Dietary Fiber	4 g	14%
Total Sugars	12 g	—
Protein	9 g	18%
Vitamin A	0.4 mcg	4%
Vitamin C	30 mg	150%
Vitamin D	0.18 mcg	—
Potassium	298 mg	3.2%
Calcium	1144 mg	90%
Iron	0.5 mg	2%

Greek Vegetable Omelet

Prep time: 5 minutes
Cook time: 5 minutes
Total time: 10 minutes

LEVEL 3: MODERATE

....

This Greek-inspired omelet is the ideal start to your feeding period. Loaded with countless nutrients and plenty of protein, it will leave you feeling full and energized. Take your pick from the various add-ons, although I'm partial to the olives, feta, and mint—authentic Greek flavors.

....

MAKES 2 SERVINGS

For the omelet
4 large eggs
2 tablespoons fat-free milk
½ teaspoon paprika
¼ teaspoon allspice
½ teaspoon salt
½ teaspoon black pepper
1½ teaspoons extra-virgin olive oil

Add-ons
½ cup crumbled feta cheese
½ cup halved cherry tomatoes
⅓ cup drained marinated
   artichoke hearts
3 tablespoons chopped fresh
   parsley
3 tablespoons chopped fresh mint
2 tablespoons pitted kalamata
   olives

1. In a medium bowl, whisk together all the omelet Ingredients except the olive oil.

2. Coat a 10-inch nonstick skillet with the olive oil and set it over medium-high heat.

3. Once the oil is shimmering, pour the egg mixture into the skillet and stir it with a spatula for 5 seconds.

4. Push the cooked egg in from the edge of the skillet to the center and tilt the pan to allow the uncooked egg to fill in the empty spots.

5. Cook the omelet for 1 minute, until the eggs are set, then remove it from the heat. Spoon your desired add-ons onto one side of the omelet and use a spatula to fold the remaining half of the omelet over the add-ons.

6. Slice the omelet into two portions. Serve with warm pita bread, if desired.

NUTRITION	Per Serving	% of Daily Value
Calories	320	—
Total Fat	22 g	28%
Saturated Fat	9.4 g	47%
Polyunsaturated Fat	6.7 g	—
Monounsaturated Fat	7.5 g	—
Trans Fat	0.04 g	—
Cholesterol	405 mg	135%
Sodium	520 mg	23%
Total Carbohydrates	11 g	4%
Dietary Fiber	4 g	14%
Total Sugars	5 g	—
Protein	20 g	40%
Vitamin A	41 mcg	4%
Vitamin C	2.8 mg	2%
Vitamin D	2 mcg	10%
Potassium	481 mg	10%
Calcium	320 mg	25%
Iron	4.2 mg	25%

Overnight Cereal in a Jar

Prep time: 5 minutes
Cook time: 0 minutes
Total time: 5 min + overnight

LEVEL 1: EASY

. . . .

Mix up this version of overnight oats the night before and enjoy it hot or cold for breakfast the next day! The cereal softens overnight, and dividing it into individual servings in lidded jars makes it easy to take breakfast with you on the run.

. . . .

MAKES 4 SERVINGS

⅔ cup **almond milk**
½ cup shelled **hemp hearts**
2 tablespoons **chia seeds**
2 teaspoons **erythritol sweetener**
   (such as Swerve)
1 teaspoon **vanilla extract**
**Berries, sugar-free chocolate
   chips, nuts, nut butter,** and/
   or **Greek yogurt**, for topping
   (optional)

1. Combine the almond milk, hemp hearts, chia seeds, sweetener, and vanilla in a bowl. Cover with a lid or plastic wrap and place in the refrigerator to chill for at least 6 hours, or overnight.

2. In the morning, add any desired toppings, such as berries, sugar-free chocolate chips, or nuts for added texture, a tablespoon of nut butter for flavor, or full-fat Greek yogurt for creaminess.

NUTRITION	Per 4 Servings	% of Daily Value
Calories	638	32%
Total Fat	48 g	69%
Saturated Fat	4.4 g	22%
Polyunsaturated Fat	36.6 g	—
Monounsaturated Fat	5.98 g	—
Trans Fat	0.03 g	—
Cholesterol	—	0%
Sodium	118 mg	6%
Total Carbohydrates	37 g	14%
Dietary Fiber	12.2 g	43%
Total Sugars	12.7 g	14%
Protein	30 g	60%
Vitamin A	117 mcg	15%
Vitamin C	1 mg	1%
Vitamin D	2 mcg	35%
Potassium	1152 mg	33%
Calcium	536 mg	67%
Iron	9 mg	62%

Almond Flour Pancakes

Prep time: 5 minutes
Cook time: 20 minutes
Total time: 25 minutes

LEVEL 1: EASY

. . . .

These hearty pancakes will satisfy your craving for a sweet and easy breakfast. Remember that the finer the almond flour, the closer the result will be to your expectations of "real" pancakes.

. . . .

MAKES 4 SERVINGS

1 heaping cup finely ground
    almond flour
2 tablespoons erythritol
    sweetener (such as Swerve)
1 teaspoon baking powder
⅛ teaspoon salt
2 large eggs
⅓ cup unsweetened coconut milk
1 tablespoon coconut oil
½ teaspoon vanilla extract
Unsalted butter, for frying

1. Combine all the Ingredients in a large bowl and mix well to form a smooth batter.

2. Heat a large skillet over medium-low heat and add ½ teaspoon of butter. When the butter is melted, drop ¼ cup batter onto the pan for each pancake. Cook until bubbles form around the edges, then flip and cook for an additional 1–2 minutes, or until evenly browned.

3. Repeat with the remaining batter, adding more butter to the skillet as needed. You should end up with a total of 6–8 pancakes. Serve warm with butter and sugar-free syrup.

NUTRITION	Per Serving	% of Daily Value
Calories	243	12%
Total Fat	21 g	31%
Saturated Fat	8 g	38%
Polyunsaturated Fat	3.5 g	—
Monounsaturated Fat	8.7 g	—
Trans Fat	0.1 g	—
Cholesterol	93 mg	31%
Sodium	239 mg	12%
Total Carbohydrates	12.3 g	5%
Dietary Fiber	3 g	11%
Total Sugars	1.5 g	2%
Protein	8.3 g	17%
Vitamin A	40 mcg	5%
Vitamin C	—	—
Vitamin D	0.5 mcg	10%
Potassium	210 mg	6%
Calcium	140 mg	17%
Iron	1.5 mg	11%

Chicken Mini Frittatas

Prep time: 15 minutes
Cook time: 30 minutes
Total time: 45 minutes

LEVEL 3: MODERATE

. . . .

Comfort food isn't just for nighttime! These Chicken Mini Frittatas transform any dull morning into an energized start to the day. Loaded with protein and healthy fats, this recipe also makes the perfect dish to serve at your next brunch. Feel free to swap out the herbs or add in veggies to make your own twist.

. . . .

MAKES 4 SERVINGS

1 pound skinless boneless chicken
    breast
2 medium eggs
½ cup almond flour
1 cup shredded mozzarella
    cheese
2 tablespoons finely chopped
    fresh basil
2 tablespoons chopped chives
2 tablespoons chopped parsley
½ teaspoon garlic powder
Sea salt and black pepper,
    to taste
1 tablespoon olive oil
Ranch dressing, for serving

1. Chop the uncooked chicken breast into tiny pieces, and then place the pieces in a large mixing bowl.

2. Stir in the almond flour, eggs, mozzarella, basil, chives, parsley, garlic powder, salt, and pepper. Mix well to combine.

3. Add the oil to a large nonstick pan and heat over medium-low heat. Scoop the chicken mixture into the pan, then slightly flatten to create a frittata. Cook the frittatas in batches, about 4 per batch.

4. Fry at medium-low temperature until golden brown on both sides, about 6–8 minutes.

5. Serve with ranch dressing.

NUTRITION	Per Serving	% of Daily Value
Calories	357	18%
Total Fat	21 g	30%
Saturated Fat	6.2 g	31%
Polyunsaturated Fat	3 g	—
Monounsaturated Fat	9.8 g	—
Trans Fat	0.02 g	—
Cholesterol	187 mg	62%
Sodium	383 mg	19%
Total Carbohydrates	4.2 g	2%
Dietary Fiber	1.8 g	6%
Total Sugars	0.7 g	1%
Protein	37 g	75%
Vitamin A	219 mcg	27%
Vitamin C	5.2 mg	7%
Vitamin D	0.56 mcg	11%
Potassium	545 mg	16%
Calcium	198 mg	25%
Iron	1.63 mg	12%

LUNCH

Rustic Avocado and Corn Salad

Prep time: 10 minutes
Cook time: 0 minutes
Total time: 10 minutes

LEVEL 1: EASY

. . . .

Here's the perfect light meal for lunch that you can easily customize to your own taste and preferences. High in calcium and fiber, it can be made in a matter of minutes and served with your favorite chicken or fish.

. . . .

MAKES 2 SERVINGS

2 avocados, diced
2 medium red onions, diced
2 cups cherry tomatoes
2 cups sweet corn
1 cup feta cheese
2 tablespoons finely chopped
    fresh cilantro
2 tablespoons finely chopped
    fresh parsley
2 tablespoons Italian dressing
1 lime, juiced
Salt, to taste
Pepper, to taste

1. Arrange the avocado, onion, tomatoes, corn, and feta cheese in 2 medium bowls, giving each Ingredient its own section and filling in all the gaps.

2. Sprinkle the cilantro and parsley over the top. Drizzle the dressing and the lime juice over the salad, then season with salt and pepper to taste.

3. Serve with grilled chicken or salmon, or with our own favorite, the Caprese Chicken on page 32.

NUTRITION	Per Serving
Calories	422 kcal
Total Carbohydrates	18 g
Protein	40 g
Total Fat	29 g
Saturated Fat	8 g
Polyunsaturated Fat	18 g
Monounsaturated Fat	9 g
Trans Fat	4 g
Cholesterol	45 mg
Sodium	298 mg
Potassium	17 mg
Dietary Fiber	21 g
Sugars	9 g
Vitamin A	45%
Vitamin C	23%
Calcium	28%
Iron	22%

Caprese Chicken

Prep time: 10 minutes
Cook time: 25 minutes
Total time: 35 minutes

LEVEL 3: MODERATE

. . . .

This is a pretty straightforward recipe, with basic Ingredients. It's destined to become your favorite summertime dinner. The chicken is prepared with olive oil, salt, pepper, and Italian seasoning. If you don't have Italian seasoning, just substitute equal parts garlic powder, dried basil, and dried oregano instead.

. . . .

MAKES 4 SERVINGS

2 tablespoons olive oil, divided
2 pounds boneless, skinless
    chicken breasts
1 teaspoon salt
1 teaspoon black pepper
1 teaspoon chili powder
1 tablespoon dried Italian
    seasoning
1 teaspoon sweet paprika
8 thick slices ripe tomato
8 (1-ounce) slices fresh mozzarella
    cheese
8 medium basil leaves
4 tablespoons balsamic glaze or
    balsamic reduction

1. Preheat the oven to 350°F.

2. Heat a large cast-iron pan over medium heat and add 1 tablespoon of the olive oil.

3. While your oil is heating up, butterfly the chicken: cut each chicken breast from the side about three-quarters of the way through, then open the chicken and lay flat.

4. Rub each chicken breast with the remaining 1 tablespoon of olive oil and season with the salt, pepper, chili powder, Italian seasoning, and sweet paprika.

5. Place 2 slices of tomato, 2 slices of mozzarella cheese, and 2 basil leaves on one side of each chicken breast. Close the chicken breasts and use toothpicks to help keep them closed around the filling.

6. Transfer the stuffed chicken breasts to the pan and sear for about 5 minutes on each side, until golden brown.

7. Transfer the pan to the oven until the internal temperature reaches 165°F.

8. Transfer the chicken breasts to a plate and let rest 3–5 minutes.

9. Slice into ¼-inch slices and drizzle the balsamic glaze over the top of the chicken. Serve over your favorite salad: we suggest the Rustic Avocado and Corn Salad on page 31.

NUTRITION	Per Serving
Calories	366 kcal
Total Carbohydrates	4 g
Protein	35 g
Total Fat	12 g
Saturated Fat	5 g
Polyunsaturated Fat	3 g
Monounsaturated Fat	5 g
Trans Fat	—
Cholesterol	85 mg
Sodium	387 mg
Potassium	23 mg
Dietary Fiber	1 g
Sugars	2 g
Vitamin A	35 % Daily Value
Vitamin C	15 % Daily Value
Calcium	15 % Daily Value
Iron	10% Daily Value

Mediterranean Quiche

Prep time: 10 minutes
Cook time: 25 minutes
Total time: 35 minutes

LEVEL 3: MODERATE

....

Pop a bite of this quiche in your mouth for instant satisfaction! Most—if not all—of these Ingredients are already in your kitchen, which makes this lunch a great way to use up what you already have. The key Ingredient is the cream cheese, which enhances the velvety texture of the filling.

....

MAKES 6 SERVINGS

1 cup whole-wheat flour

½ teaspoon salt

⅓ cup unsalted butter, softened

4 eggs, beaten

1 cup shredded mozzarella cheese

3 tablespoons chopped chives

1 tablespoon cream cheese

1 teaspoon dried oregano

½ teaspoon ground paprika

1. Preheat the oven to 365°F.

2. Whisk together the flour and salt in the bowl of a stand mixer fitted with the dough attachment, then add the butter and mix until the dough pulls away from the sides of the bowl without leaving much of a sticky residue.

3. Roll out the dough between two sheets of parchment until it is 12 inches round and about ¼ inch thick. Remove the top piece of parchment. Transfer the dough with the bottom parchment paper to a 9-inch round pie pan and gently press the dough into the pan. Bake for 10 minutes, until golden.

4. While baking, whisk the eggs, mozzarella, chives, cream cheese, oregano, and paprika together in a medium bowl.

5. Remove the crust from the oven and place it into the refrigerator for 5 minutes.

6. Pour the egg-cheese mixture into the crust, spreading it into an even layer, and bake for 10 minutes, until golden. Remove from the oven and allow to cool for 5 minutes.

7. Slice and serve immediately, or chill the quiche for 4–6 hours before serving. Refrigerate leftovers in an airtight container for up to three days.

NUTRITION	Per Serving	% of Daily Value
Calories	220	
Total Fat	10 g	13%
Saturated Fat	5.6 g	28%
Polyunsaturated Fat	0.9 g	—
Monounsaturated Fat	3.2 g	—
Trans Fat	—	—
Cholesterol	130 mg	43%
Sodium	190 mg	8%
Total Carbohydrates	17 g	6%
Dietary Fiber	1 g	4%
Total Sugars	1 g	—
Protein	12 g	24%
Vitamin A	195 mcg	20%
Vitamin C	0.9 mg	—
Vitamin D	0.7 mcg	4%
Potassium	105 mg	2%
Calcium	213 mg	15%
Iron	1.8 mg	10%

Broccoli and Pork Latkes

Prep time: 10 minutes
Cook time: 20 minutes
Total time: 30 minutes

LEVEL 3: MODERATE

. . . .

*This meal has all the nutrients
you could ask for, including
fiber and antioxidants from the
broccoli and protein from the
pork. Crispy on the outside,
soft on the inside, these latkes
are the perfect recipe to use up
any leftovers. If using leftover
cooked meat instead of ground
pork, just be sure to shred it
first!*

. . . .

MAKES 4 SERVINGS

1 cup shredded **broccoli**
½ cup ground **pork**
3 tablespoons **whole-wheat flour**
1 tablespoon **Italian seasoning**
1 tablespoon dried **dill**
1 teaspoon **salt**
2 **eggs**, beaten
1 teaspoon **extra-virgin olive oil**

1. Combine the broccoli and pork in a mixing
bowl, then add the flour, Italian seasoning, dill,
and salt, mixing until combined.

2. Stir in the eggs, mixing until smooth.

3. Heat the olive oil in a skillet over medium-high
heat.

4. Spoon ½ cup of the mixture per latke into the
skillet and cook for 4 minutes on each side, or
until golden.

5. Drain the latkes on paper towels, then serve!

NUTRITION	Per Serving	% of Daily Value
Calories	120	
Total Fat	7 g	9%
Saturated Fat	2 g	10%
Polyunsaturated Fat	0.8 g	—
Monounsaturated Fat	3.1 g	—
Trans Fat	—	—
Cholesterol	70 mg	23%
Sodium	200 mg	9%
Total Carbohydrates	8 g	3%
Dietary Fiber	1 g	4%
Total Sugars	—	—
Protein	8 g	16%
Vitamin A	139 mcg	15%
Vitamin C	2.5 mcg	2%
Vitamin D	0.52 mcg	2%
Potassium	152 mg	4%
Calcium	52 mg	4%
Iron	1.5 mg	8%

Pasta Frittata

Prep time: 15 minutes
Cook time: 15 minutes
Total time: 30 minutes

LEVEL 3: MODERATE

. . . .

If you have leftover pasta of any kind, this is the recipe you'll want to reference! This dish is endlessly versatile, 100 percent foolproof, and good for you, too. Eggs are a good source of protein, heart-healthy unsaturated fats, and important nutrients, such as vitamins B$_6$, B$_{12}$, and D. Whole milk is also loaded with essential nutrients including vitamin D, phosphorous, calcium, B vitamins, and protein. Moreover, it may help inhibit osteoporosis, prevent bone fractures, and help you regulate your weight. Don't be afraid to experiment by substituting your own favorite cheeses and seasonings for the cheddar and spices below. There's simply no way to mess this one up!

. . . .

MAKES 3 SERVINGS

1 cup whole milk
3 eggs, beaten
2 ounces cheddar cheese, shredded
1 teaspoon salt
1 teaspoon chopped fresh dill
¼ teaspoon crushed red pepper flakes

¼ teaspoon paprika
¼ teaspoon ground black pepper
2 ounces cooked tagliatelle pasta or linguine pasta (follow package instructions and cook to al dente)
1 teaspoon extra-virgin olive oil

---

1. Preheat the oven to 360°F.

2. Whisk together the milk, eggs, cheese, salt, dill, crushed red pepper flakes, paprika, and pepper in a large bowl. Using a spatula, mix in the cooked pasta.

3. Coat an oven-safe skillet with the olive oil, then pour the frittata batter into the skillet and spread it into an even layer.

4. Bake for 15 minutes, until golden brown. Remove from the oven, then chill for 10 minutes in the refrigerator before slicing and serving.

NUTRITION	Per Serving	% of Daily Value
Calories	230	—
Total Fat	11 g	14%
Saturated Fat	6.1 g	31%
Polyunsaturated Fat	0.5 g	—
Monounsaturated Fat	3.9 g	—
Trans Fat	—	—
Cholesterol	25 mg	8%
Sodium	190 mg	8%
Total Carbohydrates	18 g	7%
Dietary Fiber	1 g	3%
Total Sugars	6 g	—
Protein	14 g	28%
Vitamin A	222 mcg	25%
Vitamin C	11.9 mcg	15%
Vitamin D	3.35 mcg	15%
Potassium	551 mg	10%
Calcium	351 mg	25%
Iron	0.8 mg	4%

Stuffed Portobello Mushrooms

Prep time: 10 minutes
Cook time: 15 minutes
Total time: 25 minutes

LEVEL 3: MODERATE

. . . .

These creamy stuffed mushroom caps are ideal for busy days when you don't have much time in the kitchen. Chock-full of vitamin D, protein, and antioxidants.

. . . .

MAKES 4 SERVINGS

2 Portobello mushrooms

2 tablespoons extra-virgin olive oil

2 ounces artichoke hearts, drained and chopped

1 tablespoon coconut cream

1 tablespoon cream cheese

1 tablespoon chopped fresh cilantro

1 teaspoon minced garlic

1 cup steamed spinach, chopped

3 ounces cheddar cheese, shredded

½ teaspoon salt

½ teaspoon ground black pepper

1. Preheat the oven to 360°F and line a baking sheet with parchment paper.

2. Drizzle the portobello mushrooms with olive oil, then place them onto the prepared baking sheet. Bake for 5 minutes, until juices leak out. Remove from the oven.

3. Combine the artichoke hearts, coconut cream, cream cheese, cilantro, and garlic in a large bowl. Mix in the spinach, cheddar cheese, salt, and pepper.

4. Stuff the mushrooms with the cheese mixture and bake for an additional 5–8 minutes, or until the cheese melts. Remove from the oven and allow to cool on the pan for 5 minutes.

5. Cut each mushroom in half and serve.

NUTRITION	Per Serving	% of Daily Value
Calories	140	—
Total Fat	11 g	14%
Saturated Fat	4 g	20%
Polyunsaturated Fat	0.9 g	—
Monounsaturated Fat	5.8 g	—
Trans Fat	—	—
Cholesterol	10 mg	3%
Sodium	360 mg	16%
Total Carbohydrates	7 g	3%
Dietary Fiber	2 g	7%
Total Sugars	2 g	—
Protein	6 g	12%
Vitamin A	290 mcg	30%
Vitamin C	17.2 mg	20%
Vitamin D	0.12 mcg	—
Potassium	328 mg	6%
Calcium	136 mg	10%
Iron	0.4 mg	4%

Garlic Beef Salpicao

Prep time: 15 minutes
Cook time: 15 minutes
Total time: 30 minutes

LEVEL 3: MODERATE

. . . .

*This savory dish packs a
flavorful punch! Worcestershire
sauce, lime juice, and chili
peppers costar with garlic in this
anything-but-typical steak. Be
sure to cook the garlic in warm,
not hot, butter to maximize its
aroma and infuse the butter with
garlicky goodness.*

. . . .

MAKES 2 SERVINGS

1 pound **boneless ribeye steak,**
    cut into thin strips
1 tablespoon **Worcestershire sauce**
1 tablespoon **lime juice**
½ teaspoon **salt**
½ teaspoon **chili pepper**
2 tablespoons **unsalted butter**
2 **garlic cloves,** diced
1 tablespoon **sour cream**

1. Place the steak strips in a medium mixing bowl and add the Worcestershire sauce, lime juice, salt, and chili powder and massage the mixture into the steak, then set aside to marinate for 15 minutes.

2. Heat the butter in a large skillet over medium-high heat.

3. Add the garlic and cook for 2 minutes. Add the marinated steak and cook for 2 minutes per side, or until it begins to brown.

4. Stir in the sour cream and cover the skillet with a lid. Cook for 10 minutes, stirring occasionally to incorporate all the flavors. Remove from the heat and allow to cool for 3 minutes.

5. Transfer to a platter and serve.

NUTRITION	Per Serving	% of Daily Value
Calories	390	—
Total Fat	14 g	18%
Saturated Fat	6.2 g	31%
Polyunsaturated Fat	0.7 g	—
Monounsaturated Fat	7.3 g	—
Trans Fat	—	—
Cholesterol	125 mg	42%
Sodium	540 mg	23%
Total Carbohydrates	3 g	1%
Dietary Fiber	1 g	—
Total Sugars	—	—
Protein	52 g	104%
Vitamin A	122 mcg	15%
Vitamin C	30.5 mg	35%
Vitamin D	0.32 mcg	2%
Potassium	994 mg	20%
Calcium	35 mg	2%
Iron	5.6 mg	30%

Mediterranean Tuna Salad

Prep time: 5 minutes
Cook time: 0 minutes
Total time: 5 minutes

LEVEL 1: VERY EASY

. . . .

Mediterranean cuisine places a lot of emphasis on seafood for protein, rather than red meat. Not only is there more variety when it comes to seafood, there are also more health benefits! Tuna is packed with vitamin D, which may fight disease, regulate mood, and support weight loss. Pair it with savory olives and tangy red wine vinegar, and this recipe will renew your faith in salads.

. . . .

MAKES 1 SERVING

1 (5-ounce) can tuna in water, drained
6 lettuce leaves, chopped
½ cup whole cherry tomatoes
¼ cup sliced kalamata olives
¼ cup cilantro
1 tablespoon red wine vinegar
1 tablespoon extra-virgin olive oil
½ teaspoon salt
½ teaspoon black pepper

1. Combine all the Ingredients in a serving bowl, tossing to combine.

2. Serve with toast or pita bread, if desired.

NUTRITION	Per Serving	% of Daily Value
Calories	270	—
Total Fat	8 g	10%
Saturated Fat	1.1 g	6%
Polyunsaturated Fat	1.9 g	—
Monounsaturated Fat	10 g	—
Trans Fat	0.005 g	—
Cholesterol	35 mg	12%
Sodium	420 mg	18%
Total Carbohydrates	8 g	3%
Dietary Fiber	—	23%
Total Sugars	—	—
Protein	16 g	32%
Vitamin A	470 mcg	110%
Vitamin C	72 mg	6%
Vitamin D	0.9 mcg	4%
Potassium	181 mg	4%
Calcium	22 mg	2%
Iron	1.5 mg	8%

Italian Turkey Sandwich

Prep time: 10 minutes
Cook time: 0 minutes
Total time: 10 minutes

LEVEL 1: VERY EASY

. . . .

*Craving a holiday meal without
the unwanted bloating? This
Italian Turkey Sandwich is your
answer! The savory turkey and
salty mozzarella drizzled with
balsamic vinegar are what
sandwich dreams are made of.
Feel free to swap out the deli
slices if you have leftover turkey
at home.*

. . . .

MAKES 1 SERVING

2 slices whole-wheat bread
2 deli meat turkey breast slices
2 slices mozzarella cheese
1 cup arugula
2 tablespoons sliced kalamata
olives
2 tablespoons sliced sun-dried
tomatoes
1 teaspoon Italian seasoning
1 teaspoon balsamic vinegar

1. Place a slice of whole-wheat bread on a serving plate, then top with 1 slice of turkey and 1 slice of mozzarella.

2. Add the remaining slices of turkey and mozzarella, then layer the arugula, olives, and sun-dried tomatoes on top.

3. Sprinkle with the Italian seasoning and drizzle with balsamic vinegar. Place the second slice of bread on top. Serve immediately.

NUTRITION	Per Serving	% of Daily Value
Calories	430	—
Total Fat	16 g	21%
Saturated Fat	7 g	35%
Polyunsaturated Fat	77.7 g	—
Monounsaturated Fat	126 g	—
Trans Fat	—	—
Cholesterol	50 mg	17%
Sodium	1070 mg	43%
Total Carbohydrates	42 g	15%
Dietary Fiber	6 g	21%
Total Sugars	6 g	—
Protein	29 g	58%
Vitamin A	262 mcg	50%
Vitamin C	61 mg	8%
Vitamin D	0.3 mcg	2%
Potassium	552 mg	10%
Calcium	489 mg	40%
Iron	4.1 mg	25%

Italian Caprese Toast

Prep time: 5 minutes
Cook time: 0 minutes
Total time: 5 minutes

LEVEL 2: EASY

. . . .

If you grow your own produce, I highly recommend using garden-fresh tomatoes and basil for this recipe. This simple yet satisfying meal makes the perfect lunch or appetizer. Easy to make and quick to devour, this seasonal snack will make its way into your weekly rotation in no time!

. . . .

MAKES 4 SERVINGS

4 slices whole-wheat bread, toasted

4 ounces mozzarella cheese, sliced

1 cup halved cherry tomatoes

¼ cup loosely packed whole basil leaves

1 teaspoon dried oregano

Sea salt, to season

Black pepper, to season

2 tablespoons balsamic vinegar glaze

1. Place the toasted bread on a serving platter. Top each bread slice with a slice of mozzarella and some tomatoes, basil, and oregano.

2. Season with salt and pepper, and drizzle each serving with ½ tablespoon of balsamic vinegar glaze. Serve immediately.

NUTRITION	Per Serving	% of Daily Value
Calories	190	—
Total Fat	8 g	10%
Saturated Fat	4 g	20%
Polyunsaturated Fat	1.2 g	—
Monounsaturated Fat	2.2 g	—
Trans Fat	—	—
Cholesterol	20 mg	7%
Sodium	300 mg	13%
Total Carbohydrates	20 g	7%
Dietary Fiber	3 g	11%
Total Sugars	3 g	—
Protein	10 g	20%
Vitamin A	36 mcg	15%
Vitamin C	57 mg	6%
Vitamin D	0.15 mcg	—
Potassium	229 mg	4%
Calcium	165 mg	15%
Iron	1.4 mg	8%

Avocado and Chickpea Salad

Prep time: 10 minutes
Cook time: 0 minutes
Total time: 10 minutes

LEVEL 1: VERY EASY

. . . .

It just doesn't get tastier than this vegan dish! The flavorful combination, loaded with plant-based protein and fiber, will leave you feeling light and satisfied. It's perfect for a family gathering or picnic, so keep this salad in mind during the summer months and al fresco dining.

. . . .

MAKES 4 SERVINGS

1 (15-ounce) can chickpeas, drained

1 large cucumber, sliced

1 cup whole cherry tomatoes

1 ripe avocado, sliced

¼ cup tightly packed fresh parsley leaves

1 tablespoon extra-virgin olive oil

Juice of ½ large lemon

Sea salt, to season

Black pepper, to season

1. Combine the chickpeas, cucumber, tomatoes, avocado, and parsley in a medium bowl.

2. Add the olive oil, lemon juice, salt, and black pepper to the salad mixture, stirring to combine. Serve and enjoy!

NUTRITION	Per Serving	% of Daily Value
Calories	270	—
Total Fat	14 g	18%
Saturated Fat	1.7 g	9%
Polyunsaturated Fat	0.6 g	—
Monounsaturated Fat	1.3 g	—
Trans Fat	0.002 g	—
Cholesterol	—	—
Sodium	320 mg	14%
Total Carbohydrates	31 g	11%
Dietary Fiber	11 g	39%
Total Sugars	6 g	—
Protein	9 g	18%
Vitamin A	3.5 mcg	2%
Vitamin C	26 mg	2%
Vitamin D	—	—
Potassium	587 mg	10%
Calcium	73 mg	6%
Iron	1.9 mg	10%

Lemon and Herb Roasted Chicken with Potatoes

Prep time: 10 minutes
Cook time: 40 minutes
Total time: 1 hour

SF NF GF EF DF

LEVEL 3: MODERATE

. . . .

This one-dish meal is a showstopper. Simply gather your ingredients, chop them up, and let the oven do the rest. The zesty garlic, bright lemon, and refreshing cilantro elevate your typical chicken and potatoes into a Mediterranean classic. Loaded with protein and fiber, this recipe is a satisfying way to refuel!

. . . .

MAKES 6 SERVINGS

2¼ pounds boneless, skinless
    chicken breast, cubed
2 pounds potatoes, cut into
    ½-inch pieces
Juice of 1 lemon
2 tablespoons extra-virgin olive oil
½ cup chopped fresh cilantro
10 garlic cloves, chopped
1 tablespoon salt
1 teaspoon black pepper

1. Preheat the oven to 400°F and coat a baking dish with nonstick cooking spray.

2. Place the cubed chicken breast and potatoes into the prepared baking dish.

3. Whisk together the lemon juice, olive oil, cilantro, garlic, salt, and black pepper in a bowl. Pour the mixture over the chicken and potatoes.

4. Cover the baking dish with aluminum foil and bake for 30 minutes.

5. Remove the aluminum foil and place the baking dish back in the oven for an additional 10 minutes, until the potatoes are golden and cooked through.

6. Remove the baking dish from the oven and allow to cool for 10 minutes. Serve warm. Refrigerate leftovers in an airtight container for up to 3 days.

NUTRITION	Per Serving	% of Daily Value
Calories	340	—
Total Fat	4.5 g	6%
Saturated Fat	0.9 g	5%
Polyunsaturated Fat	0.7 g	—
Monounsaturated Fat	1.1 g	—
Trans Fat	0.012 g	—
Cholesterol	120 mg	40%
Sodium	1250 mg	54%
Total Carbohydrates	32 g	12%
Dietary Fiber	4 g	14%
Total Sugars	2 g	—
Protein	42 g	84%
Vitamin A	6.2 mcg	4%
Vitamin C	134 mg	40%
Vitamin D	0.05 mcg	—
Potassium	1300 mg	30%
Calcium	42 mg	4%
Iron	2 mg	10%

Salmon and Spinach Salad

Prep time: 10 minutes
Cook time: 10 minutes
Total time: 20 minutes

LEVEL 3: MODERATE

. . . .

Boost your heart and brain health with the fresh spinach and tender salmon fillets in this salad, which are tossed with creamy avocado and sharp red onion for a delicious contrast. Ideal for al fresco dining and family gatherings, this is an impressive dish that's easy enough to serve even when you're in a time crunch!

. . . .

MAKES 3 SERVINGS

For the salad
2 tablespoons extra-virgin olive oil
2 (6-ounce) salmon fillets
½ teaspoon salt
¼ teaspoon black pepper
4 cups baby spinach
2 tomatoes, chopped
1 avocado, diced
1 cucumber, sliced
¼ cup chopped red onion
1 tablespoon capers, drained

For the dressing
Juice of 1 lemon
1 tablespoon extra-virgin olive oil
½ teaspoon salt
¼ tablespoon black pepper

1. To make the salad, heat the olive oil in a skillet over medium-high heat.

2. Sprinkle the salmon fillets with the salt and pepper and add them to the skillet. Cook for 4–5 minutes on one side, then flip the salmon fillets over and cook for 3 minutes more, until the fish flakes easily with a fork. Remove from the heat and set aside.

3. Divide the baby spinach, tomatoes, avocado, cucumber, red onion, and capers between three serving bowls. Slice the salmon fillets and divide into three servings, topping the salad.

4. To make the dressing, whisk together all the Ingredients. Pour the dressing over the salmon before serving.

NUTRITION	Per Serving	% of Daily Value
Calories	540	—
Total Fat	33 g	42%
Saturated Fat	5.09 g	25%
Polyunsaturated Fat	4.13 g	—
Monounsaturated Fat	8.3 g	—
Trans Fat	0.079 g	—
Cholesterol	100 mg	33%
Sodium	830 mg	36%
Total Carbohydrates	15 g	5%
Dietary Fiber	7 g	25%
Total Sugars	5 g	—
Protein	47 g	94%
Vitamin A	638 mcg	20%
Vitamin C	26 mcg	30%
Vitamin D	24.8 mcg	140%
Potassium	1604 mg	35%
Calcium	81 mg	6%
Iron	2.83 mg	15%

Garlic Beef
with String Beans

Prep time: 10 minutes
Cook time: 25 minutes
Total time: 40 minutes

LEVEL 4: CHALLENGING

. . . .

The antioxidant-rich string beans add crunch and texture to this family favorite, which we serve weekly in our household. For a lunch loaded with vitamins, fiber, and protein, you just can't go wrong with this recipe. It's a satisfying meal whether you're finishing your feeding period or breaking your fast!

. . . .

MAKES 6 SERVINGS

2 tablespoons **extra-virgin olive oil**
1 pound ground **beef**
1 large **onion**, chopped
1 **green chili pepper**, chopped
1 tablespoon **salt**
1 tablespoon **black pepper**
8 **garlic cloves**, chopped
1 (16-ounce) **can crushed tomatoes**
2¼ pounds **string beans**, cut into
    1½-inch pieces

1. Heat the olive oil in a deep skillet over medium-high heat.

2. Add the ground beef and cook for 5 minutes, stirring constantly and breaking the beef into smaller pieces.

3. Stir in the onions, chili pepper, salt, and pepper and cook for 5 minutes more.

4. Stir in the garlic and cook for 2 minutes, then add the crushed tomatoes and stir for 5 minutes.

5. Add the green beans, cover the skillet, and cook for 5 minutes.

6. Remove from the heat and allow to cool for 5 minutes before serving. Refrigerate leftovers in an airtight container for up to 3 days.

NUTRITION	Per Serving	% of Daily Value
Calories	300	—
Total Fat	17 g	22%
Saturated Fat	5.2 g	26%
Polyunsaturated Fat	1.2 g	—
Monounsaturated Fat	8.3 g	—
Trans Fat	0.51 g	—
Cholesterol	70 mg	23%
Sodium	1510 mg	66%
Total Carbohydrates	16 g	6%
Dietary Fiber	5 g	18%
Total Sugars	5 g	—
Protein	24 g	48%
Vitamin A	312 mcg	60%
Vitamin C	170 mg	60%
Vitamin D	0.05 mcg	—
Potassium	739 mg	15%
Calcium	109 mg	8%
Iron	4.5 mg	25%

Italian Baked Fish

Prep time: 10 minutes
Cook time: 15 minutes
Total time: 55 minutes

LEVEL 3: MODERATE

. . . .

Full of omega-3s, vitamin D, and zinc, fish are a pillar of Mediterranean cuisine. These baked fish are marinated with Italian flavors of bright lemon, earthy oregano, and garden-fresh basil, then set atop fresh bell peppers and shallots. Marinate the fillets the night before for a quick weeknight-friendly dinner.

. . . .

MAKES 6 SERVINGS

2 pounds fish fillets

1 teaspoon salt

½ teaspoon black pepper

10 garlic cloves, minced

15 basil leaves, chopped

1½ teaspoons dried oregano

1 teaspoon ground coriander

6 tablespoons extra-virgin olive oil

Juice of 1 lemon

2 red bell peppers, sliced into strips

2 shallots, sliced

1. Pat the fish fillets dry with paper towels. Sprinkle the fillets with salt and pepper on both sides.

2. Place the fillets in a large bowl and add the garlic, basil, oregano, coriander, olive oil, and lemon juice. Massage the fillets with the seasoning, ensuring the fish is evenly coated in the marinade.

3. Place the marinated fillets on a plate and cover with plastic wrap. Refrigerate for 30 minutes. Set aside the remaining marinade.

4. Preheat the oven to 450°F and coat a baking dish with nonstick cooking spray.

5. Arrange the bell peppers and shallots in the bottom of the prepared baking dish.

6. Remove the fillets from the refrigerator and arrange on top of the peppers and shallots. Pour the reserved marinade over the fish.

7. Bake for 15 minutes, or until the fish flakes easily with a fork. Remove from the oven and let sit for 5 minutes before serving warm. Refrigerate leftovers in an airtight container for up to 3 days.

NUTRITION	Per Serving	% of Daily Value
Calories	500	—
Total Fat	32 g	41%
Saturated Fat	6.1 g	31%
Polyunsaturated Fat	1.7 g	—
Monounsaturated Fat	9.9 g	—
Trans Fat	0.006 g	—
Cholesterol	50 mg	17%
Sodium	850 mg	37%
Total Carbohydrates	33 g	12%
Dietary Fiber	2 g	7%
Total Sugars	1 g	—
Protein	23 g	46%
Vitamin A	31.2 mcg	8%
Vitamin C	127 mcg	45%
Vitamin D	0.7 mcg	4%
Potassium	678 mg	15%
Calcium	55 mg	4%
Iron	3.9 mg	20%

Greek Spanakopita

Prep time: 20 minutes
Cook time: 1 hour
Total time: 1 hour 25 minutes

LEVEL 5: AMBITIOUS

. . . .

Spanakopita is a savory Greek pie made with flaky layers of phyllo dough and a comforting mixture of spinach and feta. Serve it as a side dish at a family gathering or as a quick and energizing lunch. In Greece, this dish is so popular that you'll find it in the windows of many side-street shops.

. . . .

MAKES 12 SERVINGS

For the crust

1 cup **extra-virgin olive oil**, divided

1 package frozen **phyllo pastry sheets**, thawed

1–2 tablespoons **water**

For the filling

2 cups chopped frozen **spinach**, thawed and drained

1¼ cup crumbled rennet-free **feta cheese**

2 bunches **parsley**, stems removed, leaves chopped

1 large **onion**, minced

2 **garlic cloves**, minced

4 medium **eggs**

2 tablespoons **extra-virgin olive oil**

2 teaspoons **dried dill**

1 teaspoon **black pepper**

1. Preheat the oven to 350°F and brush the bottom and sides of a baking dish with 1 tablespoon of olive oil.

2. Combine all the filling Ingredients in a bowl, mixing until well combined.

3. Place the phyllo sheets on a clean kitchen towel and cover with a clean, damp kitchen towel to keep them from drying out.

4. Line the bottom and sides of the prepared baking dish with two sheets of phyllo, allowing the phyllo to overhang the sides of the baking dish.

5. Brush the phyllo dough with 1 tablespoon of the olive oil, then add another two sheets of phyllo and brush them with more olive oil. Continue this process until you've used two thirds of the phyllo dough, coating the crust with olive oil after every two phyllo sheets.

6. Spread the spinach filling in an even layer on top of the phyllo. Top the spinach layer with the remaining phyllo sheets, again brushing with olive oil between every two sheets.

7. Brush the final layer of phyllo with olive oil, then sprinkle the water on top.

8. Fold the excess phyllo from the sides of the baking dish over the top, and brush the folded-in dough with the remaining olive oil.

9. Bake for 1 hour, until golden brown. Remove from the oven and allow to cool for 5 minutes, then transfer to a cutting board and cut into 12 squares. Serve warm. Refrigerate leftovers in an airtight container for up to 3 days.

NUTRITION	Per Serving	% of Daily Value
Calories	450	—
Total Fat	39 g	50%
Saturated Fat	10 g	50%
Polyunsaturated Fat	1.3 g	—
Monounsaturated Fat	4.1 g	—
Trans Fat	0.015 g	—
Cholesterol	75 mg	25%
Sodium	1230 mg	53%
Total Carbohydrates	22 g	8%
Dietary Fiber	2 g	7%
Total Sugars	2 g	—
Protein	10 g	20%
Vitamin A	11.8 mcg	4%
Vitamin C	37 mg	4%
Vitamin D	0.41 mcg	2%
Potassium	272 mg	6%
Calcium	205 mg	15%
Iron	2.9 mg	15%

Chicken Cacciatore

Prep time: 10 minutes
Cook time: 20 minutes
Total time: 35 minutes

LEVEL 4: CHALLENGING

· ·

Authentic cacciatore is an Italian classic! Cacciatore refers to a meal prepared "hunter style," with chicken, onions, and tomatoes. This version adds a twist—instead of a sauce, I use a delicious Mediterranean-inspired marinade for the chicken. If you're looking for a satisfying recipe for your next family lunch, look no further.

· ·

MAKES 6 SERVINGS

3 tablespoons extra-virgin olive oil, divided
2 pounds boneless, skinless chicken breast
4 garlic cloves, minced
2 teaspoons dried oregano
1 teaspoon fresh thyme
1 teaspoon sweet paprika
1 teaspoon salt
½ teaspoon black pepper
Juice of ½ lemon
1 medium onion, thinly sliced
6 small Roma tomatoes, halved
¼ cup fresh parsley
2 tablespoons chopped fresh basil leaves

1. Preheat the oven to 400°F and coat a baking dish with 1 tablespoon of the olive oil.

2. Place the chicken breasts on a cutting board and pound with a meat mallet until the chicken is ½ inch thick.

3. Whisk together the garlic, oregano, thyme, paprika, salt, pepper, lemon juice, and the remaining 2 tablespoons of olive oil in a large bowl until well combined.

4. Place the flattened chicken breasts into the bowl and massage the marinade into the chicken, coating well.

5. Arrange the onion and tomatoes in an even layer on the bottom of the prepared baking dish.

6. Place the chicken breasts on top of the onion and tomatoes and cover with aluminum foil. Bake for 10 minutes.

7. Remove the aluminum foil and set aside. Bake the chicken for an additional 8–10 minutes, until it is thoroughly cooked.

8. Remove the chicken from the oven, re-cover with the aluminum foil, and let sit for 5–10 minutes.

9. Garnish with parsley and basil and serve! Refrigerate leftovers in an airtight container for up to 3 days.

NUTRITION	Per Serving	% of Daily Value
Calories	340	—
Total Fat	21 g	27%
Saturated Fat	5 g	25%
Polyunsaturated Fat	6.6 g	—
Monounsaturated Fat	1.7 g	—
Trans Fat	0.162 g	—
Cholesterol	95 mg	32%
Sodium	980 mg	43%
Total Carbohydrates	5 g	2%
Dietary Fiber	2 g	7%
Total Sugars	3 g	—
Protein	33 g	66%
Vitamin A	12.8 mcg	4%
Vitamin C	62 mg	15%
Vitamin D	0.59 mcg	2%
Potassium	596 mg	15%
Calcium	42 mg	4%
Iron	1.8 mg	10%

Prosciutto and Pesto Sandwich

Prep time: 10 minutes
Cook time: 0 minutes
Total time: 10 minutes

LEVEL 2: EASY

. . . .

Originating from Liguria, Italy, pesto is a thick, blended herbal paste whose Ingredients can vary depending on the recipe. I suggest testing out this dish with a variety of different pestos to see which you enjoy most. My family always prefers one with extra cheese and garlic!

. . . .

MAKES 1 SERVING

1 tablespoon **pesto**
1 loaf **whole-wheat ciabatta bread**
½ cup halved **cherry tomatoes**
½ cup drained **artichoke hearts**
½ cup **prosciutto**
½ cup **arugula**

1. Cut the ciabatta bread in half horizontally, then spread ½ tablespoon of pesto onto the cut side of each half.

2. Layer the cherry tomatoes on the bottom half and top with the artichoke hearts, prosciutto, and arugula. Place the remaining half of the bread on top.

3. Push a wooden skewer into the sandwich to make it easier to eat. Serve and enjoy!

NUTRITION	Per Serving	% of Daily Value
Calories	430	—
Total Fat	20 g	26%
Saturated Fat	4.02 g	20%
Polyunsaturated Fat	4.451 g	—
Monounsaturated Fat	10.4 g	—
Trans Fat	—	—
Cholesterol	75 mg	25%
Sodium	1600 mg	70%
Total Carbohydrates	44 g	16%
Dietary Fiber	5 g	18%
Total Sugars	4 g	—
Protein	37 g	74%
Vitamin A	534 mcg	35%
Vitamin C	642 mcg	30%
Vitamin D	2 mcg	10%
Potassium	25 mg	25%
Calcium	112 mg	8%
Iron	3.54 mg	20%

Summertime Salad

Prep time: 10 minutes
Cook time: 0 minutes
Total time: 10 minutes

LEVEL 2: EASY

. . . .

Perfect for summertime barbeques and al fresco dining, with a surprise crunch from nutty sunflower seeds and a bite from the red onions, this bright salad comes together simply. Mesclun greens are known to aid weight management, manage blood pressure, and improve digestion, so you'll love knowing this recipe is as healthy as it is quick to make!

. . . .

MAKES 2 SERVINGS

Juice of 1 lemon
1 tablespoon extra-virgin olive oil
1 teaspoon ground dried basil
1 teaspoon salt
½ teaspoon black pepper
4 cups mesclun greens mix
1 medium cucumber, sliced
½ medium red onion, sliced
½ cup sunflower seeds

1. Whisk together the lemon juice, olive oil, basil, salt, and black pepper in a bowl until combined.

2. Place the mesclun greens, cucumber, onion, and sunflower seeds in a large serving bowl. Add the dressing, tossing until the mesclun leaves are well coated in dressing. Serve and enjoy.

NUTRITION	Per Serving	% of Daily Value
Calories	310	—
Total Fat	25 g	32%
Saturated Fat	2.567 g	13%
Polyunsaturated Fat	0.624 g	—
Monounsaturated Fat	3.653 g	—
Trans Fat	0.003 g	—
Cholesterol	—	—
Sodium	910 mg	40%
Total Carbohydrates	16 g	6%
Dietary Fiber	6 g	21%
Total Sugars	5 g	—
Protein	10 g	20%
Vitamin A	1913 mcg	128%
Vitamin C	27 mcg	45%
Vitamin D	—	—
Potassium	747 mg	15%
Calcium	102 mg	8%
Iron	3.45 mg	20%

Chicken Souvlaki

Prep time: 10 minutes
Cook time: 10 minutes
Total time: 50 minutes

LEVEL 4: CHALLENGING

. . . .

The secret to souvlaki is that most of the work is in the prep, so you can prepare everything ahead of time and spend less than ten minutes actually cooking. This traditional Greek recipe, enriched with earthy herbs, sour lemon, and tangy tzatziki, is the perfect addition to any backyard barbeque.

. . . .

MAKES 5 SERVINGS

4 boneless, skinless chicken
   breasts, cut into 1-inch cubes
⅓ cup extra-virgin olive oil
2 tablespoons lemon juice
3 garlic cloves, minced
2 teaspoons dried oregano
1 teaspoon dried parsley
1 teaspoon sea salt
½ teaspoon black pepper
½ cup tzatziki sauce, to serve

1. Combine the chicken, olive oil, lemon juice, garlic, oregano, parsley, salt, and pepper in a bowl and toss to combine.

2. Cover with plastic wrap and chill for a minimum of 30 minutes.

3. Heat your grill to medium-high and thread the chicken onto skewers.

4. Grill the chicken skewers for 3–4 minutes per side, until cooked through.

5. Place the chicken on a serving platter along with tzatziki sauce and pita bread, if desired. Serve immediately.

NUTRITION	Per Serving	% of Daily Value
Calories	390	—
Total Fat	20 g	26%
Saturated Fat	3.2 g	16%
Polyunsaturated Fat	2.4 g	—
Monounsaturated Fat	11.9 g	—
Trans Fat	0.022 g	—
Cholesterol	160 mg	53%
Sodium	560 mg	24%
Total Carbohydrates	2 g	1%
Dietary Fiber	—	—
Total Sugars	0.21 g	—
Protein	49 g	98%
Vitamin A	9.2 mcg	4%
Vitamin C	32 mg	4%
Vitamin D	0.05 mcg	—
Potassium	762 mg	15%
Calcium	22 mg	2%
Iron	1.4 mg	8%

Chili (The Keto Way)

Prep time: 10 minutes
Cook time: 1 hour
Total time: 1 hour 10 minutes

LEVEL 1: EASY

. . . .

The secret to keto chili is to leave out the beans—and the sugar, of course. Spice it up to your taste, or swap in a different type of meat for variety. If you like a chunkier chili, use canned diced tomatoes instead of the sauce and crushed tomatoes. If you're lucky enough to have leftovers, use them to make the Nachos on page 73!

. . . .

MAKES 5 SERVINGS

1 pound extra lean ground beef
1 bell pepper, chopped
1 small sweet onion, chopped
2 tablespoons garlic, minced
1 (8-ounce) can tomato sauce
1 (8-ounce) can crushed tomatoes
1 (4-ounce) can diced green chilis
2–3 tablespoons chili powder
1 teaspoon pink Himalayan salt

1. Combine the ground beef, pink Himalayan salt, bell pepper, onions, and garlic in a medium soup pot and cook, stirring, until the beef is well browned, 10–13 minutes. Drain off the grease, then return the pot to the heat.

2. Add all the remaining Ingredients, starting with just 2 tablespoons of the chili powder, and stir to completely combine. Bring to a boil, then reduce the heat to low and simmer for 30 minutes.

3. Taste the chili and adjust the seasoning with the remaining tablespoon of chili powder as needed. Cook for 15–20 minutes more.

4. Serve hot. Store leftovers in the fridge in an airtight container for up to 3 days.

NUTRITION	Per Serving	% of Daily Value
Calories	177	—
Total Fat	5.4 g	8%
Saturated Fat	2.1 g	11%
Polyunsaturated Fat	0.7 g	—
Monounsaturated Fat	2 g	—
Trans Fat	0.2 g	—
Cholesterol	56 mg	19%
Sodium	999 mg	49%
Total Carbohydrates	11.6 g	4%
Dietary Fiber	3.7 g	13%
Total Sugars	5.32 g	6%
Protein	21.8 g	44%
Vitamin A	420 mcg	52%
Vitamin C	42 mg	52%
Vitamin D	0.09 mcg	2%
Potassium	740 mg	21%
Calcium	59 mg	7%
Iron	4.22 mg	30%

Chili Nachos (Using Keto Approved Tortilla chips)

Prep time: 15 minutes
Cook time: 6 minutes
Total time: 21 minutes

LEVEL 1: EASY

. . . .

You will need to keep your eye out for keto chips. Many big-box stores now carry them alongside every other chip brand. If you're having trouble finding them, check the health-food section of the grocery store or even a health-food store, if you are lucky enough to have one around. Keto has become so popular that many premade options are now available, so ask if you can't find them!

. . . .

MAKES 2 SERVINGS

3 cups **keto tortilla chips**
1 cup shredded **cheddar cheese**
½ cup leftover **Chili** (page 70), warmed
¼ cup **salsa**
2 tablespoons **sour cream**
½ **avocado**, chopped
1 small **jalapeño**, diced

1. Preheat the oven to 375°F.

2. Spread the chips out on a baking sheet and sprinkle with the cheese. Bake until the cheese is melted and beginning to brown, 5–6 minutes.

3. Remove from the oven and transfer the chips to a serving plate. Top with warm chili. Garnish your nachos with salsa, sour cream, avocado, and jalapeño, in whatever order makes you the happiest.

NUTRITION	Per Serving	% of Daily Value
Calories	542	27%
Total Fat	35 g	50%
Saturated Fat	13.8 g	69%
Polyunsaturated Fat	6.5 g	—
Monounsaturated Fat	11.2 g	—
Trans Fat	1 g	—
Cholesterol	63 mg	21%
Sodium	744 mg	37%
Total Carbohydrates	42 g	16%
Dietary Fiber	5.6 g	20%
Total Sugars	4.5 g	5%
Protein	18.3 g	37%
Vitamin A	422 mcg	53%
Vitamin C	97 mg	121%
Vitamin D	0.34 mcg	2%
Potassium	740 mg	13%
Calcium	482 mg	60%
Iron	1.53 mg	11%

Crustless Quiche

Prep time: 20 minutes
Cook time: 30 minutes
Total time: 1 hour

LEVEL 3: MODERATE

You can use this basic quiche recipe to make endless variations. Try adding spinach, or replace the bacon with ham or sausage. Adding diced peppers or broccoli is also an easy way to boost the flavor; just add about ½ cup to the egg mixture.

MAKES 6 SERVINGS

8 slices **bacon**
2 tablespoons **butter**
1 small **onion**, diced
1 tablespoon minced **garlic**
6 large **eggs**
¾ cup **whipping cream**
½ cup shredded **Swiss cheese**
½ cup shredded **Jack cheese**

1. Preheat the oven to 375°F. Butter a 9-inch pie plate or an 8-inch-square baking dish.

2. In a large frying pan over medium-high heat, fry the bacon until crispy, about 6 minutes. Transfer to a paper towel-lined plate to cool, leaving the grease in the pan. When the bacon is cool, crumble it into small pieces.

3. Add the butter to the bacon grease and return the pan to the heat. Add the onion and garlic and sauté for 5 minutes, or until soft.

4. Whisk eggs in a large bowl. Use a slotted spoon to transfer the onion and garlic to the bowl, then add a teaspoon of the butter—bacon grease mixture. Pour in the cream and whisk until fully combined. Stir in the crumbled bacon and both cheeses, then pour into the prepared baking dish.

5. Bake for 20 minutes, or until the quiche is set. Let cool 10–15 minutes before serving.

NUTRITION	Per Serving	% of Daily Value
Calories	424	21%
Total Fat	38.4 g	55%
Saturated Fat	18.55 g	93%
Polyunsaturated Fat	3.84 g	—
Monounsaturated Fat	12.18 g	—
Trans Fat	0.52 g	—
Cholesterol	270 mg	90%
Sodium	378 mg	19%
Total Carbohydrates	3.52 g	1%
Dietary Fiber	0.21 g	1%
Total Sugars	1.86 g	2%
Protein	16.35 g	33%
Vitamin A	310 mcg	39%
Vitamin C	1.39 mg	2%
Vitamin D	1.63 mcg	33%
Potassium	192 mg	5%
Calcium	202 mg	25%
Iron	1.1 mg	8%

Chicken Soup

Prep time: 15 minutes
Cook time: 40 minutes
Total time: 55 minutes

LEVEL 1: EASY

. . . .

On cool autumn days, nothing compares to a warm bowl of chicken soup. This recipe uses salsa, cubed cheese, and cabbage, adding complexity to the dish's texture. Garnished with avocado slices, this meal keeps you satisfied and energized through your afternoon lull.

. . . .

MAKES 4 SERVINGS

4 boneless, skinless chicken
   breasts
1½ cups chunky tomato salsa
2 cups chicken bone broth
½ pound Manchego cheese,
   cubed small
1 tablespoon chopped cilantro
1 cup julienned cabbage
2 tablespoons olive oil
Salt and black pepper, to taste
1 small avocado, sliced

1. In a pan, heat the olive oil and add the chicken pieces. Cook until golden brown.

2. Place the chicken, broth, and tomato salsa in a large pot, bring to a boil, and cook for 15 minutes. Add the cabbage and cilantro and cook for another 10 minutes at low temperature. Season with salt and pepper.

3. Remove from heat. Serve, garnishing with cheese cubes and avocado.

NUTRITION	Per Serving	% of Daily Value
Calories	646	32%
Total Fat	37.5 g	54%
Saturated Fat	16.81 g	82%
Polyunsaturated Fat	2.1 g	—
Monounsaturated Fat	8.95 g	—
Trans Fat	0.52 g	—
Cholesterol	183 mg	61%
Sodium	1256 mg	63%
Total Carbohydrates	10 g	4%
Dietary Fiber	4 g	14%
Total Sugars	5 g	6%
Protein	63.5 g	127%
Vitamin A	183.3 mcg	23%
Vitamin C	11.6 mg	14%
Vitamin D	—	—
Potassium	1084 mg	31%
Calcium	565 mg	71%
Iron	1.92 mg	14%

Chicken Wraps

Prep time: 10 minutes
Total time: 10 minutes
Total time: 20 minutes

LEVEL 3: MODERATE

. . . .

*For days when you're short
on time, grill the chicken and
precut the toppings the day
before. Since putting this recipe
together takes minutes, it's
perfect for busy days. Thanks to
the high fat content, this meal
keeps you full all day long.
If you're feeling playful, try
swapping out the proteins for
your family's favorites!*

. . . .

MAKES 6 SERVINGS

6 large **lettuce leaves** (iceberg)
6 **chicken tenders**, grilled
6 slices **bacon**
6 slices **ham**
6 slices **Monterey Jack cheese**
6 slices **tomatoes**
6 slices **avocado**
1 **carrot**, julienned
¼ cup **purple cabbage**, julienned
Salt and **pepper**, to taste

1. Lay 1 lettuce leaf onto a plate and lay one piece each of ham, chicken, and cheese on top; then add tomato, avocado, carrot, and cabbage.

2. Wrap it up and use a toothpick to hold it closed, if necessary. Serve with ranch dressing or mayonnaise.

NUTRITION	Per Serving	% of Daily Value
Calories	362	18%
Total Fat	25 g	36%
Saturated Fat	10 g	50%
Polyunsaturated Fat	2.7 g	—
Monounsaturated Fat	10.3 g	—
Trans Fat	0.04 g	—
Cholesterol	93.3 mg	31%
Sodium	867 mg	43%
Total Carbohydrates	4.7 g	2%
Dietary Fiber	2.3 g	8%
Total Sugars	1.7 g	2%
Protein	29 g	58%
Vitamin A	597 mcg	75%
Vitamin C	7.2 mg	9%
Vitamin D	0.5 mcg	10%
Potassium	535 mg	15%
Calcium	226 mg	28%
Iron	1.03 mg	7%

Garlic Shrimp

Prep time: 15 minutes
Cook time: 10 minutes
Total time: 25 minutes

LEVEL 1: EASY

. . . .

This is another one of those recipes that doesn't take much time. Perfect for crammed days, Garlic Shrimp combines the savory flavors of butter and garlic, while adding a surprising zest with lemon juice, sriracha, and chili pepper flakes. If you've ever thought shrimp were boring, this dish will prove you wrong and keep you coming back for seconds.

. . . .

MAKES 2 SERVINGS

1 pound shrimp, peeled and
    deveined
1 teaspoon salt
1 teaspoon pepper
3 tablespoons butter, divided
1 tablespoon olive oil
4 garlic cloves, minced
1 teaspoon paprika
¼ cup fumet
1 tablespoon sriracha
1 teaspoon crushed red pepper
    flakes
1 tablespoon lemon juice
1 tablespoon fresh chopped
    parsley or cilantro

1. Season the shrimp with the salt and pepper and set aside. Place a large nonstick skillet over medium heat and add 1 tablespoon of butter and the olive oil. Add the shrimp and sauté 1 minute. Add the minced garlic and paprika to the shrimp, stir to combine, and cook the shrimp for 1 minute. Then add the fumet and sriracha. Reduce the sauce for 1 minute, making sure not to overcook the shrimp.

2. Pour 1 tablespoon of the lemon juice over the top of the cooked shrimp. Remove the shrimp from heat, garnish with the parsley, lemon slices, and crushed red pepper. Serve with cauliflower rice or zucchini noodles.

NUTRITION	Per Serving	% of Daily Value
Total Fat	25.6 g	37%
Saturated Fat	12 g	59%
Polyunsaturated Fat	1.95 g	—
Monounsaturated Fat	10.34 g	—
Trans Fat	—	—
Cholesterol	410 mg	137%
Sodium	1691 mg	85%
Total Carbohydrates	6.43 g	2%
Dietary Fiber	1.39 g	2%
Total Sugars	2 g	2%
Protein	47.5 g	95%
Vitamin A	516 mcg	64%
Vitamin C	11 mg	14%
Vitamin D	—	—
Potassium	781 mg	22%
Calcium	176 mg	22%
Iron	2 mg	15%

Gouda Kale Pork

Prep time: 15 minutes
Cook time: 55 minutes
Total time: 1 hour 10 minutes

LEVEL 3: MODERATE

....

If you need a show-stopping dish for your upcoming dinner party, this is it! With such a unique combination of flavors and textures, you're sure to wow the crowd. The delicate sauce, made with vegetable stock, kale, and creamy Gouda, can be poured over a number of meats, including turkey and chicken.

....

MAKES 4 SERVINGS

4 pork loins (7 ounces each)
Salt and cracked black pepper,
   to taste
2 teaspoons olive oil
2 tablespoons butter
6 garlic cloves, finely minced
1 small yellow onion, minced
1 teaspoon crushed chili flakes
⅓ cup vegetable stock
1¾ cups heavy cream
3 cups kale
1 teaspoon Italian seasoning
¼ cup Gouda cheese
1 tablespoon chopped parsley

1. Season the pork with the salt and pepper on both sides and set aside. In a large pan, heat the oil over medium-high heat. Sear the pork in the hot pan for 3–5 minutes on each side, depending on the thickness, or until cooked three-fourths of the way. Remove the pork from the pan and set aside.

2. Melt the butter in the same pan in the remaining cooking juices. Add the garlic, onion, and crushed red pepper and stir-fry for 2 minutes. Add in the vegetable stock, and allow time to reduce a little.

3. Reduce heat to low, add the heavy cream, and bring the creamy sauce to a simmer. Add salt and pepper to taste.

4. Add the kale leaves and allow to wilt in the sauce, then stir in the Gouda cheese. Cook for another 3 minutes. Return the pork to the pan, add the parsley, and cook for 2 minutes. Serve.

NUTRITION	Per Serving	% of Daily Value
Calories	713	36%
Total Fat	55 g	79%
Saturated Fat	31.4 g	157%
Polyunsaturated Fat	3.06 g	—
Monounsaturated Fat	16.41 g	—
Trans Fat	1.39 g	—
Cholesterol	244 mg	81%
Sodium	415 mg	21%
Total Carbohydrates	10.5 g	2%
Dietary Fiber	1.39 g	4%
Total Sugars	4.3 g	5%
Protein	45 g	90%
Vitamin A	2036 mcg	254%
Vitamin C	62.7 mg	78%
Vitamin D	2.33 mcg	47%
Potassium	1041 mg	30%
Calcium	227 mg	28%
Iron	2 mg	14%

Meat and Broccoli Casserole

Prep time: 20 minutes
Cook time: 30 minutes
Total time: 50 minutes

LEVEL 3: MODERATE

. . . .

Serve at a family gathering or meal-plan your way to leftovers with this hearty Meat Casserole. Thanks to this recipe, I've gotten over my fear of droopy, soggy cabbage casseroles! Made with simple Ingredients, this dish is quick to whip up and will leave everyone at the table full and satisfied.

. . . .

MAKES 5 SERVINGS

3 tablespoons olive oil
2 pounds lean ground beef
1 medium onion, finely chopped
¼ teaspoon black pepper
1 tablespoon minced garlic
1 teaspoon cumin
2 teaspoons salt
1 tablespoon mustard
¼ cup mayonnaise
1½ cups shredded sharp cheddar
2 cups broiled broccoli

1. Preheat the oven to 400°F. Grease a baking dish with olive oil.

2. Heat a large skillet over medium-high heat and add the olive oil, then add the onions and beef. Cook for 5 minutes, stirring to undo large chunks, until the beef is browned and the onion is tender.

3. Add in the black pepper, garlic, cumin, and salt. Cook, stirring for a few minutes more.

4. Remove from heat. Add the mayonnaise, mustard, and one cup of cheddar. Mix well.

5. Transfer the mixture to the prepared baking dish. Sprinkle with the remaining cheese.

6. Bake until the cheese is golden brown and the casserole is heated through, about 15 minutes.

7. Remove from the oven and let it cool for 10 minutes. Serve with ½ cup of broccoli on the side.

NUTRITION	Per Serving	% of Daily Value
Calories	632.5	32%
Total Fat	46.8 g	67%
Saturated Fat	15.9 g	80%
Polyunsaturated Fat	7.03 g	—
Monounsaturated Fat	19.07 g	—
Trans Fat	1.29 g	—
Cholesterol	151 mg	50%
Sodium	1372 mg	69%
Total Carbohydrates	6.3 g	2%
Dietary Fiber	1.51 g	5%
Total Sugars	1.7 g	2%
Protein	45.6 g	91%
Vitamin A	205 mcg	26%
Vitamin C	31.4 mg	43%
Vitamin D	0.38 mcg	8%
Potassium	774 mg	22%
Calcium	295 mg	37%
Iron	4.9 mg	35%

Broccoli Salad (Keto Friendly)

Prep time: 20 minutes
Cook time: 15 minutes
Total time: 35 minutes

LEVEL 1: EASY

. . . .

Thanks to keto's carb restrictions, bland salads are usually a no-go. This simple, classic Broccoli Salad is one of my favorite side dishes. Made with bacon, cashews, red onions, and topped with a tangy, creamy dressing, you'll wonder why you didn't experiment more with broccoli before starting keto!

. . . .

MAKES 2 SERVINGS

8 slices of raw **bacon**
½ large **broccoli head**
1 large **carrot**, grated
¼ small **red onion**
1 small **red bell pepper**, chopped
¼ cup **cashews**
1 **tomato**, diced

For the dressing
½ cup **mayonnaise**
½ cup **sour cream**
1 tablespoon **lemon juice**
Salt and cracked **black pepper**,
   to taste

1. Preheat the oven to 400°F and line a large oven tray with parchment paper.

2. Place the bacon on the prepared tray.

3. Bake for 10 minutes, then reduce the heat to 350°F and bake for 8 minutes more.

4. Remove the bacon from the oven and let it cool, then cut into small pieces.

5. In a bowl, whisk together all the dressing Ingredients; add salt and pepper. Set aside in the refrigerator.

6. To soften the broccoli, set a medium pot of salted water on the stove and bring to a boil. Cut the broccoli into bite-sized florets. Place the florets in the water and cook for 3 minutes; drain and let broccoli cool.

7. Grate the carrot and the onion and place in a large bowl.

8. Dice the red bell pepper and chop the cashews, place in the bowl with the carrot and onion.

9. Add the bacon, broccoli, and tomato to the bowl and mix. Add the dressing and mix well to combine.

NUTRITION	Per Serving	% of Daily Value
Calories	1029	51%
Total Fat	99 g	143%
Saturated Fat	25.7 g	128%
Polyunsaturated Fat	33 g	—
Monounsaturated Fat	34 g	—
Trans Fat	0.52 g	—
Cholesterol	94 mg	31%
Sodium	979 mg	49%
Total Carbohydrates	18.9 g	7%
Dietary Fiber	3.5 g	12%
Total Sugars	8.9 g	10%
Protein	18.3 g	37%
Vitamin A	2174 mcg	272%
Vitamin C	72.8 mg	91%
Vitamin D	0.4 mcg	8%
Potassium	762 mg	22%
Calcium	94.5 mg	12%
Iron	2.2 mg	16%

Chicken Salad Wrap

Prep time: 10 minutes
Total time: 10 minutes
Total time: 20 minutes

LEVEL 1: EASY

. . . .

I first had chicken salad with nuts and sour cream when I was in college, and it was a game-changer for me. These Ingredients make a perfect chicken salad that is filled with healthy fats and is creamy and delicious. You can bake the chicken for this salad with a sweet and spicy Piri Piri spice or use your favorite rotisserie chicken from the grocery store.

. . . .

MAKES 5 SERVINGS

1½ pounds cold cooked chicken
½ cup sour cream
5 tablespoons sugar-free
   mayonnaise
3 tablespoons lemon juice
1 stalk celery, finely chopped
⅓ cup chopped walnuts
2 teaspoons chopped chives
¼ teaspoon garlic powder
10 lettuce leaves

1. Cube the chilled chicken and place in a large serving bowl. Add all the remaining Ingredients and stir until the chicken is fully coated.

2. Serve cold on the lettuce leaves or a wrap of your choice. Refrigerate and store for up to 3 days.

NUTRITION	Per Serving	% of Daily Value
Calories	485	24%
Total Fat	34 g	49%
Saturated Fat	7.9 g	40%
Polyunsaturated Fat	13.75 g	—
Monounsaturated Fat	9.7 g	—
Trans Fat	0.24 g	—
Cholesterol	78 mg	26%
Sodium	335 mg	17%
Total Carbohydrates	23 g	9%
Dietary Fiber	9.74 g	35%
Total Sugars	6.7 g	7%
Protein	27.8 g	56%
Vitamin A	15444 mcg	1931%
Vitamin C	70 mg	87%
Vitamin D	0.22 mcg	4%
Potassium	1607 mg	46%
Calcium	292 mg	37%
Iron	7 mg	46%

DINNER

Mackerel and Tomato Spaghetti

Prep time: 10 minutes
Cook time: 20 minutes
Total time: 30 minutes

LEVEL 4: AMBITIOUS

. . . .

Rich in omega-3, mackerel is a common protein source for people from the Mediterranean. You can use fresh or canned, depending on what's more convenient for you. If you choose fresh, note that you'll need to add olive oil, salt, and pepper along with the fish in step 2.

. . . .

MAKES 2 SERVINGS

4 ounces whole-wheat spaghetti

2 (4-ounce) cans mackerel packed in oil, or 8 ounces fresh mackerel

2 garlic cloves, minced

2 cups halved cherry tomatoes

1 large red bell pepper, seeded and diced

10 green olives, pitted and roughly chopped

Salt and pepper, to taste

1 handful of parsley, chopped

Juice of 1 lemon

1. Cook the spaghetti in a pot of salted boiling water according to the package directions, then drain and set aside.

2. If using fresh mackerel, combine the fish with 5 tablespoons olive oil, 1 teaspoon salt, and ½ teaspoon ground black pepper in a skillet over medium-high heat. Cook for 10–15 minutes, turning once halfway through, until golden brown. If using canned mackerel, place the mackerel along with its oil in a skillet over medium-high heat.

3. Add the garlic and cook for 2–3 minutes, until golden brown.

4. Add the tomatoes, bell pepper, olives, salt, and pepper and cook for 10 minutes, until the bell peppers and tomatoes are tender.

5. Transfer the spaghetti to the skillet and cook for 1 minute, until the spaghetti is heated through.

6. Remove from the heat, garnish with the parsley, and drizzle with the lemon juice before serving.

NUTRITION	Per Serving	% of Daily Value
Calories	560	—
Total Fat	20 g	36%
Saturated Fat	4.1 g	21%
Polyunsaturated Fat	3.1 g	—
Monounsaturated Fat	10.9 g	—
Trans Fat	—	—
Cholesterol	46 mg	15%
Sodium	851 mg	35%
Total Carbohydrates	71.2 g	25%
Dietary Fiber	7.5 g	30%
Total Sugars	11.5 g	—
Protein	22.2 g	51%
Vitamin A	857 mcg	83%
Vitamin C	140 mcg	234%
Vitamin D	10.55 mcg	20%
Potassium	1030 mg	22%
Calcium	76 mg	8%
Iron	3.4 mg	19%

Italian Chicken

Prep time: 5 minutes
Cook time: 25 minutes
Total time: 30 minutes

LEVEL 4: CHALLENGING

. . . .

*Poultry is a popular
Mediterranean Diet protein,
since it contains nutrients that
protect against heart disease,
cancer, and diabetes. Here,
meaty mushrooms, crisp white
wine, and acidic tomatoes give
seasoned chicken an Italian
makeover.*

. . . .

MAKES 4 SERVINGS

2 **chicken breasts**, halved
   lengthwise
2 teaspoons **salt**, divided
2 teaspoons **pepper**
2 tablespoons **extra-virgin
   olive oil**, divided
1 **onion**, diced
1 (15-ounce) **can diced tomatoes**,
   undrained
½ cup sliced **mushrooms**
3 **garlic cloves**, minced
½ cup **white wine**
1 tablespoon **lemon juice**
1 teaspoon **Italian seasoning**
½ cup chopped **parsley**

1. Generously season the chicken breasts with
1 teaspoon of the salt and the pepper.

2. Heat 1 tablespoon of the olive oil in a skillet
over medium-high heat. Add the chicken breasts
and cook for 2–3 minutes per side, until browned
on both sides. Remove from the skillet, transfer to
a plate, and cover to keep warm.

3. Add the onions to the skillet over medium-high
heat and cook for 3–5 minutes, until they become
translucent.

4. Add the tomatoes, mushrooms, garlic, white
wine, lemon juice, Italian seasoning, and the
remaining 1 teaspoon salt and cook, covered,
for 15–20 minutes, stirring periodically.

5. Add the parsley and return the chicken to the
skillet. Cook for 8–10 minutes, until the chicken
has reached an internal temperature of 165°F.

6. Remove from the heat and divide between four
serving bowls.

NUTRITION	Per Serving	% of Daily Value
Calories	292	—
Total Fat	14 g	22%
Saturated Fat	2 g	13%
Polyunsaturated Fat	8.1 g	—
Monounsaturated Fat	0.5 g	—
Trans Fat	—	—
Cholesterol	76 mg	24%
Sodium	1041 mg	45%
Total Carbohydrates	11 g	4%
Dietary Fiber	3 g	13%
Total Sugars	5 g	—
Protein	26 g	52%
Vitamin A	188 mcg	19%
Vitamin C	26 mcg	32%
Vitamin D	0.2 mcg	1%
Potassium	730 mg	21%
Calcium	96 mg	10%
Iron	2 mg	11%

Chicken Penne

Prep time: 10 minutes
Cook time: 20 minutes
Total time: 30 minutes

LEVEL 5: AMBITIOUS

. . . .

Penne is the plural form of the Italian word penna, *meaning "feather" or "pen." The pasta got its name because back when it was invented, its shape resembled a fountain pen's steel nibs. This creamy recipe takes penne to new heights with chicken thighs—which are loaded with iron and zinc, thanks to their higher percentage of dark meat. Serve with garlic bread if you're feeling traditional.*

. . . .

MAKES 4 SERVINGS

1½ pounds chicken thighs
1 teaspoon Italian seasoning
1 teaspoon salt
¼ teaspoon ground black pepper
¼ cup extra-virgin olive oil, divided
½ onion, chopped
⅔ cup chopped sun-dried tomatoes
4 garlic cloves, minced
3 cups low-sodium chicken broth
8 ounces penne
3 cups fresh spinach
½ cup heavy cream
¼ cup grated Parmesan cheese
2 tablespoons chopped fresh parsley
2 tablespoons lemon juice

1. Season the chicken thighs with the Italian seasoning, salt, and pepper.

2. Heat 2 tablespoons of the olive oil in a deep nonstick skillet over medium-high heat. Add the chicken thighs and cook for 3–4 minutes per side, until golden brown.

3. Transfer the chicken thighs to a plate and set aside.

4. Heat the remaining 2 tablespoons olive oil in the same skillet over medium-high heat. Add the onions and cook for 4–5 minutes, until translucent.

5. Stir in the sun-dried tomatoes and garlic and cook for 1 minute, until fragrant.

6. Add the chicken broth and penne and bring to a boil. Cook for 10–12 minutes, then decrease the heat to medium-low and return the chicken thighs to the pot.

7. Cook, covered, for 8–10 minutes or until the pasta is tender, stirring occasionally.

8. Add the spinach, heavy cream, and Parmesan to the skillet, stirring to combine.

9. Remove from the heat and divide between four serving bowls. Garnish with the parsley and drizzle with the lemon juice, then serve.

NUTRITION	Per Serving	% of Daily Value
Calories	820	—
Total Fat	54 g	80%
Saturated Fat	16 g	103%
Polyunsaturated Fat	14.7 g	—
Monounsaturated Fat	20.1 g	—
Trans Fat	1 g	—
Cholesterol	213 mg	71%
Sodium	887 mg	39%
Total Carbohydrates	57 g	19%
Dietary Fiber	5 g	21%
Total Sugars	9 g	—
Protein	42 g	84%
Vitamin A	598 mcg	58%
Vitamin C	16 mcg	19%
Vitamin D	0.4 mcg	2%
Potassium	1298 mg	37%
Calcium	174 mg	17%
Iron	5 mg	28%

Moroccan Chicken

Prep time: 5 minutes
Cook time: 25 minutes
Total time: 30 minutes

LEVEL 4: CHALLENGING

· ·

*Moroccans love sweetening
their dishes with dried fruits,
including dates and apricots.
Here the dried fruit enhances
the chicken's sauce, balancing
the spice from the jalapeño.
Topped with almonds for crunch
and laid upon a bed of nutty
couscous, this chicken is as
authentic as it gets!*

· ·

MAKES 4 SERVINGS

¼ cup all-purpose flour
1 teaspoon salt, divided
⅛ teaspoon ground black pepper
1½ pounds boneless, skinless
   chicken thighs
1 tablespoon extra-virgin olive oil
1 medium yellow onion, thinly
   sliced
1 tablespoon minced jalapeño
1 garlic clove, minced
2 teaspoons Moroccan spice
1 cup low-sodium chicken broth
½ cup halved dried dates
½ cup chopped dried apricots
1 (15-ounce) can chickpeas,
   drained and rinsed
1 teaspoon red wine vinegar
2 cups cooked couscous
2 tablespoons sliced almonds

1. Whisk the all-purpose flour, ¾ teaspoon of the salt, and the pepper together in a shallow baking dish.

2. Dry the chicken thighs with paper towels and dredge both sides in the seasoned flour.

3. Heat the olive oil in a nonstick skillet over medium-high heat. Add the chicken thighs and cook for 3–4 minutes per side, until golden, then transfer to a plate and set aside.

4. Add the onions to the skillet, still over medium-high heat, and cook for 5–7 minutes, until they are translucent and golden.

5. Add the jalapeño, garlic, and Moroccan spice and cook for 1 minute, until the garlic is fragrant.

6. Stir in the chicken broth, dates, and apricots, then transfer the chicken back to the skillet and decrease the heat to medium-low. Cook, stirring occasionally, for 10 minutes.

7. Add the chickpeas, red wine vinegar, and remaining ¼ teaspoon of salt. Stir well and remove from the heat.

8. Divide the couscous between four serving bowls and top with the chicken and sauce. Garnish each serving with the sliced almonds.

NUTRITION	Per Serving	% of Daily Value
Calories	631	
Total Fat	16.02 g	23%
Saturated Fat	2.87 g	14%
Polyunsaturated Fat	3.45 g	—
Monounsaturated Fat	7.33 g	—
Trans Fat	0.03 g	—
Cholesterol	159.89 mg	53%
Sodium	981 mg	49%
Total Carbohydrates	73.38 g	30%
Dietary Fiber	10.46 g	37%
Total Sugars	30.75 g	—
Protein	46.22 g	92%
Vitamin A	210 mcg	25%
Vitamin C	4.15 mcg	5%
Vitamin D	0.04 mcg	—
Potassium	1082 mg	31%
Calcium	99.72 mg	12%
Iron	3.92 mg	28%

Baked Salmon with Sage

Prep time: 10 minutes
Cook time: 20 minutes
Total time: 30 minutes

LEVEL 4: CHALLENGING

. . . .

*Sage holds an exalted place
in the history of alternative
medicine, having been featured
in a cure for the plague and
used to ward off evil. Its
culinary usage dates back to
the fourteenth century. Today,
sage is a popular herb in Italian
cuisine for seasoning fish.
Peppery sage contrasts with the
savory salmon here to create
an appetizing, protein-packed
dinner.*

. . . .

MAKES 5 SERVINGS

2½ pounds **salmon**
1 teaspoon **salt**
½ teaspoon ground **black pepper**
2 small **lemons**, thinly sliced
2 cups halved **cherry tomatoes**
½ cup **artichoke hearts**
½ cup **olives**
¼ **red onion**, sliced
3 sprigs fresh **sage**
1 **jalapeño**, seeded and chopped
2 teaspoons **capers**
¼ cup **extra-virgin olive oil**

1. Preheat the oven to 400°F and line a baking sheet with parchment paper.

2. Season the salmon with the salt and pepper. Arrange the salmon on the prepared baking sheet, tucking the thinner end of the fillet under so it will cook evenly.

3. Layer the lemon slices, tomatoes, artichokes, olives, red onion, sage, jalapeño, and capers on top of and around the salmon. Drizzle the olive oil over the salmon and bake for 20 minutes, until the salmon has a bright pink color and flakes easily with a fork.

4. Remove from the oven and allow to cool for 3 minutes before serving. Refrigerate leftovers in an airtight container for up to 3 days.

NUTRITION	Per Serving	% of Daily Value
Calories	422	—
Total Fat	27 g	35%
Saturated Fat	6 g	30%
Polyunsaturated Fat	6 g	—
Monounsaturated Fat	13 g	—
Trans Fat	1 g	—
Cholesterol	114 mg	38%
Sodium	317 mg	14%
Total Carbohydrates	6 g	2%
Dietary Fiber	2 g	7%
Total Sugars	2 g	—
Protein	39 g	78%
Vitamin A	94 mcg	10%
Vitamin C	7 mcg	8%
Vitamin D	—	—
Potassium	1097 mg	25%
Calcium	46 mg	4%
Iron	2 mg	10%

Mediterranean Beef Tacos

Prep time: 10 minutes
Cook time: 20 minutes
Total time: 30 minutes

LEVEL 4: CHALLENGING

. . . .

This recipe merges Mediterranean and Mexican cuisines using seasoned ground beef enhanced with Mediterranean favorites such as olives, sun-dried tomatoes, and roasted bell peppers, then topped with all the classic fixings. As with most of these recipes, you can work with what you've got on hand—pantry loaded with canned beans? Toss them in! Feel free to experiment with the Ingredients; with a recipe this delicious, you just can't lose.

. . . .

MAKES 12 SERVINGS

1 pound 90 percent lean
  ground beef
1 tablespoon chili powder
1 teaspoon ground cumin
¾ teaspoon salt
½ teaspoon dried oregano
½ teaspoon garlic powder
¼ teaspoon ground black pepper
½ cup sliced and pitted green
  olives
¼ cup chopped drained sun-dried
  tomatoes

¼ cup chopped roasted red bell peppers
½ cup tomato sauce
¼ cup water
12 (6-inch) whole-wheat tortillas, warmed
1 cup shredded 4-cheese blend or Mexican cheese
  blend
1 cup shredded lettuce
1 small red onion, diced
2 tablespoons chopped fresh cilantro

---

1. Place the ground beef in a large skillet over medium-high heat.

2. Cook for 6–8 minutes, breaking the beef into smaller pieces with a spoon, until there is no pink left.

3. Add the chili powder, cumin, salt, oregano, garlic powder, and pepper, stirring to combine.

4. Add the olives, sun-dried tomatoes, and roasted red bell peppers, stirring to combine, and cook for 2 minutes, until the bell peppers soften.

5. Decrease the heat to medium-low and add the tomato sauce and water. Cook for 7–8 minutes, until some of the liquid has evaporated. Remove from the heat.

6. Arrange the tortillas on a serving platter and add 2 tablespoons of the ground beef mixture to each.

7. Top with the cheese, lettuce, red onion, and cilantro before serving. Refrigerate leftovers in an airtight container for up to 3 days.

NUTRITION	Per Serving	% of Daily Value
Calories	233	
Total Fat	7.55 g	16%
Saturated Fat	3.122 g	17%
Polyunsaturated Fat	0.838 g	—
Monounsaturated Fat	2.947 g	—
Trans Fat	0.083 g	—
Cholesterol	32 mg	—
Sodium	561 mg	37%
Total Carbohydrates	26.81 g	11%
Dietary Fiber	2 g	8%
Total Sugars	2.94 g	—
Protein	14.61 g	27%
Vitamin A	568 mcg	24%
Vitamin C	7 mcg	8%
Vitamin D	3 mcg	1%
Potassium	320 mg	7%
Calcium	136 mg	14%
Iron	3.04 mg	17%

Roasted Red Pepper Mac and Cheese

Prep time: 5 minutes
Cook time: 20 minutes
Total time: 25 minutes

LEVEL 5: AMBITIOUS

. . . .

Who knew gluten-free mac and cheese could be so splendid? Thanks to the fiber-rich chickpea pasta in this dish, celiacs can rejoice! Here we elevate the family classic with sweet roasted red peppers, sharp red onion, and fragrant garlic to add vitamin C, vitamin B$_9$, and antioxidants, respectively, to your diet.

. . . .

MAKES 4 SERVINGS

8 ounces chickpea pasta

2 tablespoons extra-virgin olive oil

¼ cup diced red onion

1 garlic clove, minced

1 tablespoon gluten-free flour

½ cup skim milk

1 cup shredded sharp cheddar cheese

1 cup nonfat plain Greek yogurt

1 teaspoon Italian seasoning

½ teaspoon sumac

½ teaspoon ground black pepper

¼ teaspoon salt

1 cup chopped roasted red peppers

¼ cup crumbled feta cheese

1. Cook the chickpea pasta in a pot of salted boiling water for 2 minutes less than recommended by the package instructions. Drain and set aside.

2. Meanwhile, heat the olive oil in a deep skillet over medium-high heat. Add the red onion and garlic and cook for 2 minutes, until the onions start to soften.

3. Stir in the gluten-free flour and cook, stirring, for 1 minute, until fully incorporated.

4. Stir in the skim milk and cook, whisking constantly, for 5–8 minutes, until it is smooth and thickened.

5. Add ½ cup of the cheddar and stir until it melts, then stir in the remaining ½ cup of cheddar.

6. Add the Greek yogurt, Italian seasoning, sumac, pepper, and salt, and cook, stirring, for 30 seconds, until smooth.

7. Add the roasted red peppers and chickpea pasta and cook for 2 minutes, until heated through.

8. Top with the feta cheese, then serve and enjoy!

NUTRITION	Per Serving	% of Daily Value
Calories	166	
Total Fat	8.14 g	12%
Saturated Fat	3.745 g	15%
Polyunsaturated Fat	0.461 g	—
Monounsaturated Fat	3.0201 g	—
Trans Fat	0.123 g	—
Cholesterol	19 mg	7%
Sodium	224 mg	15%
Total Carbohydrates	15.02 g	6%
Dietary Fiber	2.98 g	11%
Total Sugars	3.55 g	
Protein	10.29 g	21%
Vitamin A	589 mcg	25%
Vitamin C	22.3 mcg	30%
Vitamin D	9 mcg	2%
Potassium	90 mg	2%
Calcium	140 mg	18%
Iron	2.26 mg	16%

Mediterranean Meatballs

Prep time: 10 minutes
Cook time: 20 minutes
Total time: 30 minutes

LEVEL 3: MODERATE

Make these Mediterranean Meatballs in bulk and freeze them for up to three months to save yourself time and energy on bustling weekdays. These chicken meatballs make a superb lunch dipped in tzatziki, or can be paired with your favorite salad of choice!

MAKES 4 SERVINGS

1 pound ground chicken
½ cup panko breadcrumbs
½ cup crumbled feta cheese
¼ cup minced red onions
¼ cup minced sun-dried tomatoes
¼ cup minced roasted red
   peppers
1 garlic clove, minced
1 large egg
2 tablespoons extra-virgin olive oil
½ teaspoon salt
½ teaspoon ground black pepper
¼ teaspoon dried basil
¼ teaspoon dried oregano
3 tablespoons plain Greek yogurt
1 tablespoon chopped fresh mint
   leaves

1. Preheat the oven to 400°F and line a baking sheet with parchment paper.

2. Combine the ground chicken, breadcrumbs, feta, red onions, sun-dried tomatoes, roasted red peppers, garlic, egg, olive oil, salt, pepper, basil, and oregano in a large bowl, mixing thoroughly.

3. Form the mixture into 15 meatballs, each about 2½ inches in diameter. Place them 1 inch apart on the prepared baking sheet.

4. Bake for 25–30 minutes, until golden brown.

5. Remove from the oven and transfer the meatballs to a serving platter. Top with the Greek yogurt and mint and serve!

NUTRITION	Per Serving	% of Daily Value
Calories	328	—
Total Fat	21.82 g	45%
Saturated Fat	7.043 g	—
Polyunsaturated Fat	2.928 g	—
Monounsaturated Fat	10.503 g	—
Trans Fat	0.83 g	—
Cholesterol	162 mg	—
Sodium	590 mg	39%
Total Carbohydrates	7.92 g	3%
Dietary Fiber	1 g	4%
Total Sugars	2.09 g	—
Protein	25.67 g	47%
Vitamin A	476 mcg	20%
Vitamin C	16.7 mcg	22%
Vitamin D	26 mcg	4%
Potassium	798 mg	17%
Calcium	141 mg	14%
Iron	20.2 mg	11%

Greek Salmon Fusilli

Prep time: 5 minutes
Cook time: 20 minutes
Total time: 25 minutes

LEVEL 3: MODERATE

. . . .

With its buttery, smoky flavors, flaky smoked salmon takes pasta to a heavenly Level in this Mediterranean dish, tossed with bright red onion, tangy olives, and salty feta. Serve this recipe cold or warm, with soft bread and a light salad on the side.

. . . .

MAKES 10 SERVINGS

12 ounces **fusilli** or **rotini pasta**
1½ cups flaked or cubed smoked or cooked **salmon**
1 cup halved **grape tomatoes**
1 cup **baby spinach**
1 medium **cucumber**, diced
½ cup sliced and pitted **green olives**
½ cup sliced and pitted **black olives**
½ cup crumbled **feta cheese**
¼ cup thinly sliced **red onion**
¼ cup thinly sliced **red bell pepper**
¼ cup thinly sliced **yellow bell pepper**
½ cup **extra-virgin olive oil**
½ cup **white wine vinegar**
2 **garlic cloves**, minced
2 teaspoons **Dijon mustard**
2 teaspoons dried **basil**
2 teaspoons dried **thyme**
½ teaspoon **salt**
¼ teaspoon ground **black pepper**

1. Cook the pasta in a pot of salted, boiling water according to the package instructions. Drain and rinse with cold water.

2. Combine the cooked pasta, salmon, tomatoes, spinach, cucumber, green and black olives, feta, red onion, red and yellow bell pepper in a serving bowl, tossing well.

3. Whisk together the olive oil, white wine vinegar, garlic, mustard, basil, thyme, salt, and pepper in a bowl. Drizzle the dressing over the pasta and toss to combine.

4. Serve and enjoy! Refrigerate leftovers in an airtight container for up to 3 days.

NUTRITION	Per Serving	% of Daily Value
Calories	240	
Total Fat	15.62 g	32%
Saturated Fat	3.15 g	—
Polyunsaturated Fat	1.772 g	—
Monounsaturated Fat	9.509 g	—
Trans Fat	0.022 g	—
Cholesterol	29 mg	—
Sodium	289 mg	19%
Total Carbohydrates	12.49 g	5%
Dietary Fiber	2.5 g	10%
Total Sugars	1.23 g	—
Protein	12.34 g	23%
Vitamin A	640 mcg	27%
Vitamin C	15.8 mcg	21%
Vitamin D	208 mcg	35%
Potassium	303 mg	6%
Calcium	62 mg	6%
Iron	1.04 mg	6%

Baked Lemon Salmon

Prep time: 10 minutes
Cook time: 15 minutes
Total time: 25 minutes

LEVEL 3: MODERATE

Busy cooks will fall in love with this simple and scrumptious Baked Lemon Salmon recipe. It just takes a bit of prep and the oven does the rest for you. If you're in a time crunch, marinate the fish and slice up your vegetables the night before. And wrap the salmon in foil while baking to spend even less time cleaning up!

MAKES 4 SERVINGS

¼ cup extra-virgin olive oil
Juice of 1 lemon
Zest of 1 lemon
1 teaspoon crushed red pepper flakes
1 teaspoon dried dill
1 teaspoon dried parsley
¼ teaspoon salt
⅛ teaspoon ground black pepper
4 skinless salmon fillets
2 cups halved grape tomatoes
1 cup sliced and pitted green olives
1 cup crumbled feta cheese
½ cucumber, diced
¼ cup diced red onions
¼ cup chopped artichoke hearts
¼ cup chopped fresh cilantro

1. Preheat the oven to 450°F.

2. Whisk the olive oil, lemon juice, lemon zest, crushed red pepper flakes, dill, parsley, salt, and pepper together in a small bowl.

3. Arrange the salmon fillets in a baking dish and brush them with the lemon mixture. Pour any remaining marinade onto the fillets.

4. Bake for 12–14 minutes, until flaky and tender. Remove from the oven.

5. Combine the tomatoes, olives, feta, cucumber, red onions, artichoke hearts, and cilantro in a medium bowl, mixing well.

6. Arrange the salmon fillets on four serving plates and top each with a spoonful of the tomato mixture. Serve and enjoy!

NUTRITION	Per Serving	% of Daily Value
Calories	694	
Total Fat	71.84 g	74%
Saturated Fat	10.133 g	—
Polyunsaturated Fat	4.304 g	—
Monounsaturated Fat	16.01 g	—
Trans Fat	0.115 g	—
Cholesterol	180 mg	—
Sodium	747 mg	50%
Total Carbohydrates	19.52 g	8%
Dietary Fiber	1.7 g	7%
Total Sugars	14.61 g	—
Protein	71.84 g	132%
Vitamin A	724 mcg	31%
Vitamin C	15.4 mcg	21%
Vitamin D	1389 mcg	232%
Potassium	1445 mg	31%
Calcium	234 mg	23%
Iron	2.09 mg	12%

Thyme and Carrot Chicken Soup

Prep time: 10 minutes
Cook time: 20 minutes
Total time: 30 minutes

LEVEL 4: CHALLENGING

. . . .

This Thyme and Carrot Chicken Soup is the essence of comfort—and health! It's loaded with everything you need to fight a cold: protein, vitamins, antioxidants, and fluids. Serve it during the winter months and feel confident knowing you've fueled your immune system. Pair with crusty bread or Spinach Fritters (page 11) for an even more filling meal.

. . . .

MAKES 4 SERVINGS

2 tablespoons extra-virgin olive oil

1 leek, halved lengthwise and sliced

4 garlic cloves, minced

4 carrots, peeled and sliced

3 parsnips, peeled and sliced

3 stalks celery, sliced

½ onion, diced

2 boneless, skinless chicken breasts

4 cups low-sodium chicken broth

1 cup water

2 sprigs fresh thyme

2 sprigs fresh tarragon

1 bay leaf

1 teaspoon salt

½ teaspoon ground black pepper

2 tablespoons flat-leaf parsley

1. Heat the olive oil in a pot or deep skillet over medium-high heat. Add the leek and garlic and cook for 1 minute, until the garlic is fragrant.

2. Stir in the carrots, parsnips, celery, and onion and cook for 3–4 minutes, until the vegetables soften.

3. Add the chicken breasts, chicken broth, water, thyme, tarragon, bay leaf, salt, and pepper and bring to a boil.

4. Decrease the heat to medium-low and cook, stirring occasionally, for 15 minutes.

5. Remove the chicken breasts and shred, then return the shredded chicken to the pot and cook for 2 minutes more.

6. Remove from the heat and discard the thyme and tarragon sprigs and the bay leaf. Divide the soup between four serving bowls and garnish with the parsley.

NUTRITION	Per Serving	% of Daily Value
Calories	371	—
Total Fat	12 g	15%
Saturated Fat	2 g	10%
Polyunsaturated Fat	9 g	—
Monounsaturated Fat	0.7 g	—
Trans Fat	0.002 g	—
Cholesterol	72 mg	23%
Sodium	286 mg	13%
Total Carbohydrates	36 g	13%
Dietary Fiber	8 g	29%
Total Sugars	10 g	—
Protein	31 g	62%
Vitamin A	1770 mcg	200%
Vitamin C	31.6 mcg	35%
Vitamin D	0.4 mcg	2%
Potassium	1424 mg	30%
Calcium	122 mg	12%
Iron	2.8 mg	15%

Lebanese Seasoned Shrimp

Prep time: 10 minutes
Cook time: 15 minutes
Total time: 25 minutes

LEVEL 3: MODERATE

. . . .

Spiced with coriander and parsley, simmered in white wine, and spritzed with lemon, there is nothing zestier than these Lebanese Seasoned Shrimp. Everything about this party-worthy dish is quick—with a five-minute salt cure and a fifteen-minute cook time, the biggest challenge is waiting for it to cool off before diving in!

. . . .

MAKES 2 SERVINGS

1 pound **baby shrimp**, peeled and deveined
¾ teaspoon **salt**
2 **garlic cloves**, minced
1 small **jalapeño**, seeded and minced
4 teaspoons **extra-virgin olive oil**, divided
1 tablespoon dried **coriander**
¼ cup dry **white wine**
¼ cup chopped fresh **parsley**
1 tablespoon **lemon juice**

1. Cut each shrimp in half lengthwise, then cut in half again crosswise.

2. Place the shrimp in a colander, add the salt, and massage it into the shrimp. Set the colander in the sink for 5 minutes.

3. Rinse the shrimp to remove excess salt, then combine the shrimp, garlic, and jalapeño in a bowl.

4. Heat 2 teaspoons of the olive oil in a skillet over medium-high heat.

5. Add the shrimp mixture and cook, stirring occasionally, for 3 minutes, until the shrimp are cooked through.

6. Stir in the coriander and wine, stirring occasionally for 2 minutes, until the wine has reduced by half.

7. Stir in the parsley, lemon juice, and the remaining 2 teaspoons olive oil and cook for 5 more minutes, occasionally stirring. Remove from the heat and allow to cool for 5 minutes.

8. Divide the shrimp between two serving plates and enjoy!

NUTRITION	Per Serving	% of Daily Value
Calories	300	—
Total Fat	12 g	15%
Saturated Fat	1.64 g	8%
Polyunsaturated Fat	1.77 g	—
Monounsaturated Fat	3.43 g	—
Trans Fat	0.004 g	—
Cholesterol	504 mg	168%
Sodium	970 mg	42%
Total Carbohydrates	4 g	1%
Dietary Fiber	1 g	3%
Total Sugars	2 g	—
Protein	42 g	84%
Vitamin A	73 mcg	2%
Vitamin C	6 mcg	9%
Vitamin D	—	—
Potassium	326 mg	6%
Calcium	314 mg	25%
Iron	5.23 mg	30%

Mudardara and Side Salad

Prep time: 10 minutes
Cook time: 50 minutes
Total time: 1 hour

LEVEL 4: CHALLENGING

. . . .

Lentils and rice are topped with caramelized onions in this classic Lebanese dish. You'll notice that the salad contains additional water. Following Middle Eastern tradition, the salad is poured over the mudardara, so the rice absorbs the extra liquid and becomes flavored with the lemon juice and spices. Rich in iron, folate, and protein, this dinner is a great way to fuel up before your next fast.

. . . .

MAKES 4 SERVINGS

For the mudardara
1 cup brown lentils
5 cups water, divided
1 cup rice
2 tablespoons extra-virgin olive oil
1 large onion, roughly chopped
½ tablespoon salt

For the salad
1 large tomato, diced
1 large cucumber, diced
1 medium onion, diced
1 cup chopped parsley
Juice of 1 lemon
½ cup water

1 teaspoon extra-virgin olive oil
1 tablespoon dried mint
1 teaspoon chili flakes
½ tablespoon salt

---

1. Combine the lentils and 3 cups of the water in a pot over medium-high heat. Simmer covered for 20 minutes, until the lentils become tender. Stir occasionally, if needed.

2. Add the rice and the remaining 2 cups of water and cook over low heat covered for 15–25 minutes, until the liquid has evaporated and the rice is tender. Remove the pot from the heat and set aside.

3. Heat the olive oil in a skillet over medium-high heat and add the onions and salt. Stir for 5–8 minutes, until the onions have caramelized, then remove from the heat.

4. Stir the caramelized onions and their oil into the lentil-rice mixture and set aside.

5. To assemble the salad, combine the tomato, cucumber, onion, parsley, lemon juice, water, olive oil, mint, chili flakes, and salt in a bowl.

6. Place the mudardara in a serving dish and top with the salad. Serve immediately. Refrigerate leftovers in an airtight container for up to 5 days.

NUTRITION	Per Serving	% of Daily Value
Calories	460	—
Total Fat	9 g	12%
Saturated Fat	1.3 g	7%
Polyunsaturated Fat	1.4 g	—
Monounsaturated Fat	4.2 g	—
Trans Fat	0.004 g	—
Cholesterol	—	—
Sodium	620 mg	27%
Total Carbohydrates	79 g	29%
Dietary Fiber	9 g	32%
Total Sugars	6 g	—
Protein	17 g	34%
Vitamin A	3628 mcg	160%
Vitamin C	25 mcg	30%
Vitamin D	—	—
Potassium	793 mg	15%
Calcium	122 mg	10%
Iron	5.36 mg	30%

Zucchini Noodles and Garlic Shrimp

Prep time: 10 minutes
Cook time: 10 minutes
Total time: 20 minutes

LEVEL 4: CHALLENGING

. . . .

You won't even miss traditional pasta in this flavorful recipe, which swaps in zucchini noodles for a low-carb, gluten-free version of a Mediterranean pasta dish. With savory shrimp, zesty lemon, crisp white wine, and sweet, spiraled zucchini, it's the perfect dish to serve your loved ones who may have a sensitivity to grains.

. . . .

MAKES 4 SERVINGS

4 tablespoons extra-virgin
   olive oil, divided
1 pound shrimp, peeled and
   deveined
½ tablespoon salt
1 teaspoon pepper
4 garlic cloves, minced
Juice of 1 lemon
Zest of 1 lemon
¼ cup white wine
½ teaspoon crushed red pepper
   flakes
4 medium zucchinis, ends
   trimmed and spiralized
¼ cup chopped parsley

1. Heat 2 tablespoons of the olive oil in a skillet set over medium-high heat. Add the shrimp and sprinkle the salt and pepper over the top.

2. Cook the shrimp on one side for 2 minutes, then turn over, add the garlic, and cook for 1 minute more. Transfer the shrimp and garlic to a plate and set aside.

3. Return the pan to medium-high heat and add the remaining 2 tablespoons of olive oil, along with the lemon juice, lemon zest, wine, and crushed red pepper. Stir for 3 minutes.

4. Stir in the zucchini noodles and parsley and cook for 30 seconds, until heated through.

5. Return the shrimp and garlic to the pan and cook for another minute.

6. Remove from the heat and divide the zucchini noodles and shrimp between four serving plates. Serve immediately. Refrigerate leftovers in an airtight container for up to 3 days.

NUTRITION	Per Serving	% of Daily Value
Calories	290	—
Total Fat	15 g	19%
Saturated Fat	2.08 g	10%
Polyunsaturated Fat	1.5 g	—
Monounsaturated Fat	6.12 g	—
Trans Fat	0.013 g	—
Cholesterol	280 mg	93%
Sodium	260 mg	11%
Total Carbohydrates	4 g	1%
Dietary Fiber	1 g	3%
Total Sugars	1 g	—
Protein	36 g	72%
Vitamin A	1634 mcg	40%
Vitamin C	39.2 mcg	45%
Vitamin D	—	—
Potassium	610 mg	15%
Calcium	19 mg	10%
Iron	1.54 mg	8%

Chicken, Chickpea, and Pita Salad

Prep time: 25 minutes
Cook time: 25 minutes
Total time: 1 hour 10 minutes

LEVEL 5: AMBITIOUS

. . . .

If there's one thing that makes a salad even more interesting than just delicious flavors, it's a mix of textures—and thankfully, this recipe incorporates both! Juicy chicken, velvety olive oil, crunchy red onion, and creamy feta blend together in this dish to create an exciting yet simple salad. Brimming with fiber and protein, this meal is an incredibly satisfying way to end your eating window!

. . . .

MAKES 4 SERVINGS

2 teaspoons ground sumac
1 teaspoon ground cumin
1 teaspoon dried oregano
4 tablespoons extra-virgin
 olive oil, divided
2 tablespoons lemon juice, divided
1 lemon, sliced
4 boneless, skinless chicken
 breast fillets
1 (8-inch) whole-wheat pita, sliced
1 (15-ounce) can chickpeas,
 rinsed and drained
2 cups chopped parsley
1 red onion, thinly sliced
¼ cup crumbled feta cheese

1. Combine the sumac, cumin, oregano, 1 tablespoon of the olive oil, 1 tablespoon of the lemon juice, and the lemon slices in a medium bowl.

2. Add the chicken and toss to combine. Cover with plastic wrap and refrigerate for 20 minutes.

3. When ready to cook the chicken, preheat the oven to 360°F.

4. Heat 1 tablespoon of the olive oil in a large oven-safe pan over medium-high heat.

5. Add the chicken breasts and cook for 2 minutes on each side, until both sides are lightly golden.

6. Transfer the pan to the oven and bake for 8 minutes, or until the chicken reaches an internal temperature of 165°F.

7. When the chicken is cooked through, remove the pan from the oven, loosely cover it with aluminum foil, and allow the chicken to rest for 2 minutes.

8. Heat 1 tablespoon of olive oil in another pan over medium-high heat.

9. Add the pita slices and cook for 2 minutes per side, until golden brown. Remove the pita bread from the pan and set aside.

10. Add the chickpeas to the same pan and stir for 2 minutes, until heated through. Set aside.

11. Slice the chicken and place it in a large bowl with the chickpeas, pita, parsley, onion, and feta. Toss to combine.

12. Drizzle the remaining 1 tablespoon olive oil and 1 tablespoon lemon juice over the top.

13. Divide the salad between four serving bowls and enjoy! Refrigerate leftovers in an airtight container for up to 3 days.

NUTRITION	Per Serving	% of Daily Value
Calories	540	—
Total Fat	25 g	32%
Saturated Fat	6.09 g	30%
Polyunsaturated Fat	0.96 g	—
Monounsaturated Fat	9.77 g	—
Trans Fat	0.02 g	—
Cholesterol	120 mg	40%
Sodium	35 mg	2%
Total Carbohydrates	37 g	13%
Dietary Fiber	8 g	29%
Total Sugars	7 g	—
Protein	46 g	92%
Vitamin A	623 mcg	15%
Vitamin C	41 mcg	45%
Vitamin D	0.2 mcg	—
Potassium	1076 mg	25%
Calcium	213 mg	15%
Iron	4.59 mg	25%

Spanish Chicken and Rice

Prep time: 10 minutes
Cook time: 1 hour
Total time: 1 hour 15 minutes

LEVEL 3: MODERATE

. . . .

Roasted chicken is a family favorite in my home. Thanks to some out-of-the-box thinking and Mediterranean inspiration, I transformed this classic dish using Spanish seasonings, and elevated it with pan-seared vegetables and hearty rice. This recipe is sure to make its way into your weekly rotation!

. . . .

MAKES 4 SERVINGS

¼ cup dry white wine
¼ teaspoon saffron threads
2 teaspoons salt, divided
1 teaspoon black pepper, divided
4 bone-in, skin-on chicken thighs
1 tablespoon extra-virgin olive oil
1 medium onion, finely diced
1 red bell pepper, finely diced
1 medium carrot, diced
2 tablespoons minced garlic
1 bay leaf
2 cups chicken broth
1 cup short-grain rice
¾ cup frozen peas, thawed
2 tablespoons chopped parsley

1. Preheat the oven to 375°F.

2. Combine the wine and saffron in a bowl and set aside.

3. Rub 1 teaspoon salt and ½ teaspoon pepper onto the chicken thighs, then set aside.

4. Heat the olive oil in a large oven-safe pan over medium-high heat.

5. Arrange the chicken thighs skin-side down in the pan and cook for 4 minutes, until browned. Turn the chicken over and cook for 4 more minutes, until golden brown on both sides, then transfer the chicken thighs to a plate.

6. Reduce the heat to medium-low and add the onion, bell pepper, carrot, and garlic to the pan. Cook, stirring frequently, for 5–7 minutes, until tender.

7. Stir in the wine–saffron mixture, the remaining 1 teaspoon salt and ½ teaspoon pepper, and the bay leaf.

8. Cook for 5–10 minutes, until most of the wine has evaporated, then add the chicken thighs, chicken broth, and short-grain rice and bring to a simmer.

9. Cover the pan and place it in the oven. Bake for 30 minutes, until chicken is tender and the meat pulls apart.

10. Remove the pan from the oven and stir in the peas. Allow to cool for 5 minutes.

11. Divide the chicken and rice between four serving bowls and top with parsley before serving. Refrigerate leftovers in an airtight container for up to 3 days.

NUTRITION	Per Serving	% of Daily Value
Calories	670	—
Total Fat	34.36 g	71%
Saturated Fat	9.079 g	43%
Polyunsaturated Fat	7.035 g	—
Monounsaturated Fat	14.639 g	—
Trans Fat	0.164 g	—
Cholesterol	193 mg	48%
Sodium	1247 mg	83%
Total Carbohydrates	49.86 g	20%
Dietary Fiber	3.7 g	15%
Total Sugars	3.24 g	—
Protein	37.83 g	69%
Vitamin A	3039 mcg	130%
Vitamin C	6 mg	1%
Vitamin D	6 mcg	1%
Potassium	681 mg	14%
Calcium	64 mg	6%
Iron	4.76 mg	26%

Mediterranean Turkey Casserole

Prep time: 35 minutes
Cook time: 1 hour 10 minutes
Total time: 1 hour 45 minutes

LEVEL 5: AMBITIOUS

. . . .

This protein-packed Turkey Casserole can improve bone health, regulate your metabolism, and boost energy production. Feel free to play around with the recipe; use your Thanksgiving leftovers in place of the ground turkey, or swap in whatever vegetables you have lingering in the fridge. Serve with warm pita bread on a brisk autumn evening.

. . . .

MAKES 6 SERVINGS

½ pound ground turkey
½ cup chopped green bell pepper
1 shallot, chopped
1 cup rinsed, drained, and chopped canned artichoke hearts
1 cup chopped broccoli florets
1 medium zucchini, sliced
6 large eggs
6 large egg whites
3 tablespoons fat-free milk
1 teaspoon Italian seasoning
¼ teaspoon garlic powder
¼ teaspoon black pepper
⅓ cup crumbled feta cheese

1. Preheat the oven to 350°F and coat a 9-inch-square baking dish with nonstick cooking spray.

2. Combine the ground turkey, green pepper, and shallots in a skillet over medium heat. Cook for 8–10 minutes, stirring occasionally, until there are no pink streaks remaining in the turkey.

3. Drain the turkey–veggie mixture and transfer to the prepared baking dish.

4. Arrange the artichokes, broccoli, and zucchini slices on top of the turkey.

5. Whisk the eggs, egg whites, milk, Italian seasoning, garlic powder, and pepper together in a large bowl until well combined.

6. Pour the egg mixture over the turkey–veggie mixture, then sprinkle the feta cheese on top.

7. Bake, uncovered, for 45–50 minutes, until golden.

8. Remove from the oven and allow to cool for 10 minutes.

9. Divide the casserole between six serving dishes and enjoy! Refrigerate leftovers in an airtight container for up to 3 days.

NUTRITION	Per Serving	% of Daily Value
Calories	180	—
Total Fat	9 g	12%
Saturated Fat	3.67 g	18%
Polyunsaturated Fat	1.28 g	—
Monounsaturated Fat	3.44 g	—
Trans Fat	0.039 g	—
Cholesterol	220 mg	73%
Sodium	620 mg	27%
Total Carbohydrates	7 g	3%
Dietary Fiber	3 g	11%
Total Sugars	2 g	—
Protein	17 g	34%
Vitamin A	173 mcg	10%
Vitamin C	28.9 mcg	35%
Vitamin D	0.5 mcg	1%
Potassium	332 mg	8%
Calcium	102 mg	8%
Iron	1.35 mg	8%

Classic Pepperoni Pizza

Prep time: 10 minutes
Cook time: 20 minutes
Total time: 1 hour 30 minutes

LEVEL 5: AMBITIOUS

. . . .

Sometimes nothing is more comforting than a Classic Pepperoni Pizza, seasoned with authentic Italian flavors of earthy oregano, minty basil, and savory onion powder. If you're in the mood to change things up, swap out the pepperoni for sausage, prosciutto, or bacon!

. . . .

MAKES 6 SERVINGS

For the tomato sauce
1 (12-ounce) can tomato paste
1 teaspoon dried oregano
1 teaspoon dried basil
½ teaspoon garlic powder
½ teaspoon onion powder
½ teaspoon salt
¼ teaspoon black pepper

For the crust
3¼ cups all-purpose flour, divided, plus more as needed
2 (25-ounce) envelopes active dry yeast
1 tablespoon sugar
1½ teaspoons salt
1⅓ cups warm water
⅓ cup extra-virgin olive oil

For the toppings
6 ounces low-fat pepperoni
1 cup shredded fat-free mozzarella cheese

1. Preheat the oven to 400°F.

2. To make the tomato sauce, whisk together all the Ingredients in a bowl and set aside.

3. To make the crust, whisk together 2 cups of the flour with the dry yeast, sugar, and salt in a large bowl.

4. Stir in the warm water and oil, mixing until well blended.

5. Slowly add the remaining flour a ½ cup at a time until a soft and sticky dough forms.

6. Grease the mixing bowl, transfer the dough back inside, and cover it with a kitchen towel. Let the dough rise for 1 hour or until it has doubled in size.

7. Knead the dough for 4 minutes until it is smooth and elastic, adding more flour if needed.

8. Divide the dough in half, dust your hands with flour, and press each portion of dough into a 9-inch pie pan.

9. Top each crust with the tomato sauce, pepperoni, and mozzarella. Bake the pizzas for 18–20 minutes, until the crust is browned and the cheese is bubbly.

10. Remove from the oven and allow to cool for 5 minutes. Slice each pizza into 3 slices and serve. Refrigerate leftovers in an airtight container for up to 3 days.

NUTRITION	Per Serving	% of Daily Value
Calories	490	—
Total Fat	20 g	29%
Saturated Fat	5.2 g	27%
Polyunsaturated Fat	3.35 g	—
Monounsaturated Fat	8.99 g	—
Trans Fat	0.475 g	—
Cholesterol	35 mg	12%
Sodium	1230 mg	53%
Total Carbohydrates	55 g	20%
Dietary Fiber	4 g	14%
Total Sugars	4 g	—
Protein	21 g	42%
Vitamin A	123 mcg	4%
Vitamin C	12 mcg	15%
Vitamin D	0.075 mcg	—
Potassium	349 mg	8%
Calcium	218 mg	15%
Iron	4.25 mg	25%

Vegetarian Greek Pasta

Prep time: 10 minutes
Cook time: 40 minutes
Total time: 50 minutes

LEVEL 4: CHALLENGING

. . . .

*Inspired by the rich flavors
and fragrant aromas of Greek
cuisine, this pasta is a hearty
vegetarian meal your family will
love! The creamy feta, earthy
olive oil, and roasted tomatoes
in this recipe can respectively
strengthen bones, support
weight loss, and promote heart
health.*

. . . .

MAKES 4 SERVINGS

1 cup **cherry tomatoes**
1 medium **onion**, diced
1 medium **red bell pepper**, diced
4 **garlic cloves**, minced
½ cup loosely packed fresh
    basil leaves
¼ cup loosely packed fresh
    oregano
¼ cup pitted and sliced **kalamata
    olives**
2 tablespoons **extra-virgin olive
    oil**, divided
½ tablespoon **salt**
1½ cups crumbled **rennet-free
    feta cheese**
1 teaspoon **black pepper**
1 pound dry **rigatoni pasta**

1. Preheat the oven to 350°F.

2. Combine the tomatoes, onion, bell pepper, garlic, basil, oregano, and olives in a baking dish. Drizzle with 1 tablespoon of the olive oil, sprinkle with the salt, and toss to combine.

3. Place the feta in the middle of the tomato mixture and drizzle the remaining tablespoon of olive oil on top of the cheese. Sprinkle with the black pepper.

4. Bake for 40 minutes, until the tomatoes burst. Remove from the oven and allow to cool for 5 minutes.

5. Meanwhile, cook the rigatoni pasta according to the manufacturer's instructions, reserving 1 cup of the pasta water before draining.

6. Drain the pasta and transfer to a large bowl. Mash the feta and tomato mixture with a fork and mix until combined, then add the feta-tomato sauce to the bowl with the pasta. Mix until combined, adding in the reserved pasta water if necessary.

7. Divide the rigatoni between four serving plates and enjoy! Refrigerate leftovers in an airtight container for up to 5 days.

NUTRITION	Per Serving	% of Daily Value
Calories	600	—
Total Fat	20 g	26%
Saturated Fat	8.73 g	44%
Polyunsaturated Fat	0.365 g	—
Monounsaturated Fat	1.763 g	—
Trans Fat	0.003 g	—
Cholesterol	45 mg	15%
Sodium	820 mg	36%
Total Carbohydrates	95 g	35%
Dietary Fiber	13 g	46%
Total Sugars	20 g	—
Protein	16 g	32%
Vitamin A	57 mcg	2%
Vitamin C	36 mcg	40%
Vitamin D	0.15 mcg	—
Potassium	683 mg	15%
Calcium	285 mg	20%
Iron	1.95 mg	10%

Moghrabieh with Chicken

Prep time: 10 minutes
Cook time: 1 hour 30 minutes
Total time: 1 hour 40 minutes

LEVEL 5: AMBITIOUS

Moghrabieh, known as "Lebanese couscous," is paired here with juicy, pan-seared chicken and pearl onions, and seasoned with toasty cinnamon and sweet cloves. This traditional Middle Eastern dish is rich in vitamins and minerals and is a comforting way to warm up on a winter night.

MAKES 6 SERVINGS

1 (2–3 pound) whole chicken
3 teaspoons salt, divided
1 teaspoon black pepper, divided
1 teaspoon Lebanese seven-spice blend
¼ cup plus 2 tablespoons extra-virgin olive oil, divided
2 garlic cloves
1 (2-inch) cinnamon stick
2 bay leaves
1 teaspoon whole cloves
2 cups peeled pearl onions
1 teaspoon ground cinnamon
1 teaspoon ground cumin
1 (15-ounce) can chickpeas, drained and rinsed
2 cups dry moghrabieh

1. Sprinkle the chicken with 1 teaspoon of the salt, ½ teaspoon of the pepper, and the seven-spice blend.

2. Heat 2 tablespoons of the olive oil in a large Dutch-oven pot over medium-high heat.

3. Add the chicken, breast side down, and cook for 4 minutes, until golden brown.

4. Turn the chicken over and cook for 4 minutes more, until golden on both sides.

5. Add enough water to cover the chicken, then add the garlic, cinnamon stick, bay leaves, and cloves.

6. Cook the chicken uncovered for 30 minutes, removing any fat that rises to the surface with a spoon.

7. After 30 minutes, add the pearl onions, stir to combine, and cook the chicken for another 15 minutes.

8. Whisk the cinnamon, cumin, and remaining ½ teaspoon pepper together in a bowl. Set aside one-quarter of the cinnamon mixture.

9. Add the remaining three-quarters of the spice mixture and the chickpeas to the chicken. Cook for another 10 minutes, then add the remaining 2 teaspoons salt.

10. Fill another pot with water and bring to a boil over medium-high heat. Add the dry moghrabieh and cook for 15–20 minutes, until tender.

11. Place the moghrabieh over medium-low heat and cook, stirring, for 3–4 minutes, until fluffed up.

12. Drain the moghrabieh, then return it to the pot and add the remaining ¼ cup olive oil and the reserved seasoning mixture.

13. Add a few ladles of the chicken broth to the moghrabieh and continue to cook for 7–10 minutes more, allowing the pearl couscous to absorb the chicken flavor.

14. Divide the moghrabieh between six serving bowls, adding a few ladles of the chicken broth. Add some of the chicken, onions, and chickpeas to the moghrabieh in each bowl. Serve and enjoy! Refrigerate leftovers in an airtight container for up to 3 days.

NUTRITION	Per Serving	% of Daily Value
Calories	650	—
Total Fat	34 g	43%
Saturated Fat	8.093 g	40%
Polyunsaturated Fat	1.66 g	—
Monounsaturated Fat	7.31 g	—
Trans Fat	0.153 g	—
Cholesterol	50 mg	17%
Sodium	360 mg	16%
Total Carbohydrates	50 g	18%
Dietary Fiber	10 g	36%
Total Sugars	4 g	—
Protein	38 g	76%
Vitamin A	—	—
Vitamin C	2 mcg	4%
Vitamin D	0.2 mcg	—
Potassium	363 mg	8%
Calcium	81 mg	6%
Iron	2.05 mg	10%

Zucchini Boats

. . . .

Summer always brings an abundance of zucchinis to the farmers' markets. Take advantage by making these delicious Greek-style stuffed zucchinis with a savory ground turkey filling. It's the perfect pairing of rich and delicate flavors.

. . . .

MAKES 4 SERVINGS

1 teaspoon olive oil
½ cup chopped sweet onion
1 tablespoon minced garlic
1 pound ground turkey
2 medium zucchinis, sliced in half
   lengthwise
1 (28-ounce) can diced tomatoes
½ cup pitted and chopped
   kalamata olives
1 cup crumbled feta cheese

1. Preheat the oven to 400°F.

2. Heat the olive oil in a frying pan over medium heat. Add the onion and garlic and sauté 3 minutes, until soft. Add the ground turkey and cook, stirring, 10–13 minutes, until the turkey is cooked through.

3. Meanwhile, scoop out the insides of the zucchini halves, leaving a thin layer of flesh and skin intact. Chop the zucchini insides and add to the pan with the turkey mixture. Cook for 4 minutes, until the zucchini is tender. Add half the tomatoes and all the olives. Cook just until heated through.

4. Spread the remaining half of the tomatoes on the bottom of a 9-by-13-inch baking dish. Place the zucchini halves on top, skin side down. Divide the turkey mixture between the 4 zucchini halves and top with the feta cheese.

5. Cover with foil and bake for 20 minutes, then uncover and bake for 15 minutes more, until the cheese is golden and filling is hot throughout. Serve immediately.

NUTRITION	Per Serving	% of Daily Value
Calories	464	
Total Fat	36 g	51%
Saturated Fat	10.85 g	54%
Polyunsaturated Fat	0.44 g	—
Monounsaturated Fat	2.61 g	—
Trans Fat	—	—
Cholesterol	114 mg	38%
Sodium	978 mg	49%
Total Carbohydrates	15 g	6%
Dietary Fiber	2.26 g	8%
Total Sugars	3.25 g	4%
Protein	22.6 g	45%
Vitamin A	134 mcg	17%
Vitamin C	20 mg	26%
Vitamin D	0.15 mcg	3%
Potassium	884 mg	25%
Calcium	287 mg	36%
Iron	2.96 mg	21%

Chicken and Broccoli Casserole (Keto Friendly)

Prep time: 25 minutes
Cook time: 35 minutes
Total time: 60 minutes

LEVEL 3: MODERATE

. . . .

This is a keto version of the recipe that used to be called Chicken Divan, which was made with canned cream soups and cream cheese. This version is just as creamy and decadent, but with lower sodium and without all the additives, keeping you healthy and happy!

. . . .

MAKES 8 SERVINGS

1 pound broccoli florets, steamed
    until just tender
2 cups seasoned shredded
    chicken
¼ cup chopped fresh basil
1 cup cream cheese
¾ cup whipping cream
½ cup milk
1 tablespoon Dijon mustard
1 teaspoon minced garlic
1 cup shredded cheddar cheese

1. Preheat oven to 375°F. Butter a 9-by-13-inch baking dish.

2. Combine the broccoli, chicken, and basil leaves in a bowl. Set aside.

3. Combine the cream cheese, cream, and milk in a saucepan over low heat, for about 5 minutes. Whisk in the mustard and garlic until smooth. Pour the cheese sauce over the chicken and broccoli mixture and toss to fully coat. Spread the mixture into the prepared baking dish and cover with the shredded cheese.

4. Bake for 20–30 minutes, until hot throughout and the cheese has browned. Cool for 5 minutes then serve.

NUTRITION	Per Serving	% of Daily Value
Calories	333	17%
Total Fat	28 g	40%
Saturated Fat	15.44 g	77%
Polyunsaturated Fat	2.09 g	—
Monounsaturated Fat	8.06 g	—
Trans Fat	0.78 g	—
Cholesterol	94 mg	31%
Sodium	257 mg	13%
Total Carbohydrates	7.4 g	3%
Dietary Fiber	1.57 g	6%
Total Sugars	3.54 g	4%
Protein	13.7 g	27%
Vitamin A	383 mcg	48%
Vitamin C	51.4 mg	64%
Vitamin D	0.69 mcg	14%
Potassium	338 mg	10%
Calcium	195 mg	24%
Iron	0.83 mg	6%

Turkey Burgers

Prep time: 15 minutes
Cook time: 15 minutes
Total time: 30 minutes

LEVEL 3: MODERATE

. . . .

*Savory and juicy turkey burgers
are a light alternative to ground
beef. Whether you cook them
on the grill or in a pan, these
burgers are delicious served
with all the traditional burger
toppings in a lettuce wrap, or
if you wanted to make it Keto
friendly, use a Keto friendly
cheese-bread roll. They make
a great swap for traditional
burgers at family picnics!*

. . . .

MAKES 4 SERVINGS

1 pound ground **turkey**
1 large **egg**
½ cup finely ground **almond flour**
¼ cup **sweet onion**, minced
¼ cup fresh **basil**, chopped
1 tablespoon **garlic**, minced
1 tablespoon **olive oil**
¼ tbsp **pink Himalayan salt**

1. Combine all the Ingredients in a bowl and gently mix to fully incorporate. Shape the meat mixture into 4 equal-sized patties.

2. To cook on the stovetop, heat the olive oil in a frying pan over medium-high heat. Add the burgers and cook for 4 minutes on each side, or until the turkey reaches an internal temperature of 160°F. To grill, heat the grill to medium-high. Coat the grill grates and burgers with olive oil to prevent the meat from sticking to the grates. Grill for 6–7 minutes on each side.

3. Serve immediately or refrigerate in an airtight container for up to 3 days.

NUTRITION	Per Serving	% of Daily Value
Calories	368	18%
Total Fat	31 g	44%
Saturated Fat	6.41 g	32%
Polyunsaturated Fat	2.14 g	—
Monounsaturated Fat	6.84 g	—
Trans Fat	—	—
Cholesterol	127 mg	42%
Sodium	527 mg	26%
Total Carbohydrates	5.1 g	2%
Dietary Fiber	1.66 g	6%
Total Sugars	1.05 g	1%
Protein	18.58 g	37%
Vitamin A	70 mcg	9%
Vitamin C	3.69 mg	64%
Vitamin D	0.26 mcg	5%
Potassium	294 mg	8%
Calcium	63.5 mg	8%
Iron	1.85 mg	13%

Supreme Pizza

Prep time: 20 minutes
Cook time: 20 minutes
Total time: 40 minutes

LEVEL 3: MODERATE

. . . .

This is the quick and easy way to serve pizza on Friday night, topped with all the toppings you love. Premade frozen cauliflower crusts are delicious, fast, and easy to bake in your oven. If you prefer to make your pizza crust yourself that's also a fantastic idea!

. . . .

MAKES 4 SERVINGS

1 frozen cauliflower pizza crust
½ cup sugar-free pizza sauce
1–1½ cups shredded mozzarella
  cheese
1 cup cooked and crumbled
  ground beef or Italian sausage
2 tablespoons thinly sliced
  sweet onion
2 tablespoons thinly sliced
  green pepper
2 tablespoons chopped fresh
  mushrooms

1. Preheat the oven to 425°F.

2. Place the crust on a baking sheet and bake for 10 minutes, until firm and beginning to crisp.

3. Remove from the oven and spread the sauce around the pizza crust, leaving a small border uncovered. Evenly distribute the cheese over the sauce. Sprinkle the meat and vegetables evenly over the top.

4. Bake for another 5–10 minutes, until the toppings are hot and the cheese is beginning to brown.

5. Slice the pizza into 8 pieces and serve immediately.

NUTRITION	Per Serving	% of Daily Value
Calories	363	18%
Total Fat	26 g	37%
Saturated Fat	12.71 g	64%
Polyunsaturated Fat	0.64 g	—
Monounsaturated Fat	7.08 g	—
Trans Fat	0.66 g	—
Cholesterol	143 mg	48%
Sodium	607 mg	40%
Total Carbohydrates	6.3 g	2%
Dietary Fiber	1.54 g	6%
Total Sugars	2.81 g	3%
Protein	24.7 g	49%
Vitamin A	65 mcg	8%
Vitamin C	4 mg	5%
Vitamin D	0.17 mcg	3%
Potassium	405 mg	12%
Calcium	177 mg	22%
Iron	1.86 mg	13%

Beef and Cabbage Skillet Dinner

Prep time: 20 minutes
Cook time: 45 minutes
Total time: 1 hour 5 minutes

LEVEL 3: MODERATE

. . . .

Skillet dinners were all the rage when I was a child. Make this one using a small cabbage or grab a bag of shredded coleslaw mix to make it an even quicker dinner.

. . . .

MAKES 6 SERVINGS

1½ pounds extra lean ground beef
½ sweet onion, chopped
2 tablespoons minced garlic
1 small head cabbage, chopped
1 (8-ounce) can tomato sauce
½ cup canned tomatoes and
   green chilies
⅓ cup beef broth
¼ cup red wine vinegar
Salt, to taste
Cracked black pepper, to taste

1. Combine the ground beef, onion, and garlic in a large, deep skillet over medium heat. Cook until the beef is browned, about 10–12 minutes. Drain off the grease, add all the remaining Ingredients, and stir to mix thoroughly. Bring to a boil, then reduce the heat to medium, cover, and cook for 15 minutes.

2. Remove the lid and continue to simmer until the liquid has reduced and the cabbage is soft, 5–10 minutes more. Serve hot.

NUTRITION	Per Serving	% of Daily Value
Calories	206	10%
Total Fat	6 g	9%
Saturated Fat	2.55 g	13%
Polyunsaturated Fat	0.38 g	—
Monounsaturated Fat	2.31 g	—
Trans Fat	0.25 g	—
Cholesterol	70 mg	23%
Sodium	415 mg	21%
Total Carbohydrates	11.32 g	4%
Dietary Fiber	3.69 g	13%
Total Sugars	5.61 g	6%
Protein	27 g	54%
Vitamin A	115 mcg	14%
Vitamin C	49 mg	61%
Vitamin D	0.11 mcg	2%
Potassium	764 mg	22%
Calcium	76 mg	9%
Iron	3.82 mg	27%

Beef Enchiladas

Prep time: 15 minutes
Cook time: 35 minutes
Total time: 50 minutes

LEVEL 3: MODERATE

. . . .

Make this recipe on a weekend when you have time to make each cheese "tortilla" by hand. I always suggest rolling the tortillas—I find it's easier—but you can layer them if you prefer. It's best to buy the cheese in blocks and shred it yourself for this recipe, rather than buy it pre-shredded.

. . . .

MAKES 6 SERVINGS

3 cups shredded cheddar cheese
3 cups shredded mozzarella
    cheese
3 cups shredded roast beef
    (leftover pot roast works best)
½ cup sugar-free salsa
¼ cup pickled jalapeños, drained
1 cup red enchilada sauce

1. Preheat the oven to 350°F. Butter an 8-inch-square baking dish.

2. Combine the cheddar and mozzarella. Working with 1 cup of the cheese mixture at a time, spread the cheese into an 8-inch circle in a medium nonstick frying pan, making an even, thin layer. Place the pan over low heat. The cheese should melt slowly and darken as it cooks. Continue to cook undisturbed, without checking underneath or moving in any way, until the entire circle of cheese is evenly brown throughout. Use a spatula to remove the round from the pan and set it aside to cool. Repeat with the remaining cheese to form 6 "tortillas."

3. Combine the beef and salsa in a saucepan and bring to a simmer over medium heat. Add the jalapeños and stir to combine.

4. Divide the meat mixture between the cheese tortilla rounds and gently roll. Lay rolls in the prepared baking dish and pour the enchilada sauce over the top. Bake for 8–10 minutes, until hot.

5. Serve with the lettuce, tomato, sour cream, and additional shredded cheese, if desired.

NUTRITION	Per Serving	% of Daily Value
Calories	502	25%
Total Fat	34.45 g	49%
Saturated Fat	19.5 g	98%
Polyunsaturated Fat	1.54 g	—
Monounsaturated Fat	10.11 g	—
Trans Fat	0.63 g	—
Cholesterol	139 mg	46%
Sodium	1820 mg	91%
Total Carbohydrates	6.83 g	6%
Dietary Fiber	0.28 g	1%
Total Sugars	1.17 g	1%
Protein	40 g	79%
Vitamin A	422 mcg	53%
Vitamin C	2.89 mg	4%
Vitamin D	0.58 mcg	12%
Potassium	613 mg	18%
Calcium	692 mg	87%
Iron	2.19 mg	16%

Meatloaf

Prep time: 15 minutes
Cook time: 1 hour and 30 minutes
Total time: 1 hour 45 minutes

LEVEL 3: MODERATE

This meatloaf recipe is based on an original family favorite from way back. The only difference is, I've swapped out the breadcrumbs for almond flour. No one ever notices. The best part? It's just as comforting and delicious as the one Mom used to make!

MAKES 6 SERVINGS

1 pound lean ground beef
1 pound lean ground pork
½ cup chopped sweet onion
½ cup finely ground almond flour
2 eggs, beaten
¼ cup tomato sauce
2 tablespoons Barbecue
  Seasoning
1 tablespoon brown sugar
  erythritol sweetener
  (such as Swerve)

1. Preheat the oven to 350°F. Butter a 9-by-5-inch loaf pan.

2. Combine all the Ingredients in a bowl and mix gently to just combine. Do not overmix. Press the mixture into the prepared loaf pan. Bake for 1–1¼ hours, until the meatloaf reaches an internal temperature of 160°F.

3. Allow to rest for 5 minutes, then slice and serve.

NUTRITION	Per Serving	% of Daily Value
Calories	389	19%
Total Fat	25 g	36%
Saturated Fat	7.5 g	37%
Polyunsaturated Fat	3.11 g	—
Monounsaturated Fat	11.30 g	—
Trans Fat	0.63 g	—
Cholesterol	155 mg	52%
Sodium	418 mg	21%
Total Carbohydrates	6.9 g	3%
Dietary Fiber	1.8 g	6%
Total Sugars	3.6 g	4%
Protein	33 g	66%
Vitamin A	40 mcg	5%
Vitamin C	1.29 mg	2%
Vitamin D	0.68 mcg	14%
Potassium	549 mg	16%
Calcium	53 mg	7%
Iron	3 mg	16%

Chicken Rolls

Prep time: 20 minutes
Cook time: 20 minutes
Total time: 40 minutes

LEVEL 3: MODERATE

. . . .

*Just thinking about this recipe
gets my stomach growling. Just
wait until you bite into one of
these rolls—the avocado and
cucumber slices balance the
savory flavors perfectly. And
if you're in need of leftovers,
this dish reheats nicely. Once
you've mastered this recipe,
try customizing it with different
fillings!*

. . . .

MAKES 2 SERVINGS

2 chicken breasts, flattened,
   grilled, and sliced
½ cup shredded mozzarella
   cheese
2 tablespoons minced chives
1 tablespoon lemon zest
2 tablespoons sesame seeds
½ avocado, thinly sliced
½ cucumber, sliced
2 tablespoons mayonnaise

1. Place a piece of plastic wrap on the counter.
Overlap the slices of chicken to form a rectangle.

2. Spread the mozzarella over the top of the
chicken.

3. Place the sliced avocado and cucumbers in the
center of the rectangle.

4. Top with minced chives, lemon zest, and
sesame seeds.

5. Use the plastic wrap to help you roll the
chicken. As if you are doing sushi rolls.

6. Once the rolls are ready, set them in the freezer
for 30 minutes. Cut them into 12 pieces, 2 cm
thick. Serve with mayonnaise.

NUTRITION	Per Serving	% of Daily Value
Calories	681	34%
Total Fat	47.5 g	68%
Saturated Fat	12.9 g	64%
Polyunsaturated Fat	13.72 g	—
Monounsaturated Fat	17.87 g	—
Trans Fat	0.24 g	—
Cholesterol	167.5 mg	56%
Sodium	354 mg	18%
Total Carbohydrates	6.74 g	3%
Dietary Fiber	3.7 g	13%
Total Sugars	1.35 g	2%
Protein	56.6 g	113%
Vitamin A	248 mcg	31%
Vitamin C	13.2 mg	17%
Vitamin D	1.02 mcg	20%
Potassium	792 mg	23%
Calcium	197 mg	25%
Iron	2.86 mg	20%

Chicken Parmesan Meatballs

Prep time: 15 minutes
Cook time: 35 minutes
Total time: 45 minutes

LEVEL 3: MODERATE

....

If you're a cheese lover, this dish is for you! Chicken Parmesan Meatballs are a crowd-winning twist on a classic. As opposed to lonesome ground beef meatballs, this recipe uses chicken, zucchini, and three types of cheese. In true Italian form, these meatballs are topped with marinara sauce for serving.

....

MAKES 2 SERVINGS

14 ounces ground chicken
¾ cup shredded mozzarella cheese
⅔ cup shredded Parmesan cheese
1 zucchini, shredded
1 egg
2 teaspoons white onion, diced
2 teaspoons dried minced garlic
2 teaspoons dried basil
1 teaspoon salt
1 tablespoon ground pepper
1 cup marinara sauce
½ cup shredded cheddar cheese

1. Preheat oven to 400°F. Grease a casserole dish with olive oil.

2. In a large bowl, combine all the Ingredients except for the marinara sauce and cheddar cheese, and mix thoroughly. Make about 24 meatballs and set apart.

3. In a skillet, add some olive oil and sear the meatballs. Place them in a casserole dish.

4. Bake in the oven for 20 minutes or until the meatballs are cooked through.

5. Remove from the oven and top with the sauce and cheese. Bake for another 10–15 minutes or until the cheese is melted. Serve hot.

NUTRITION	Per Serving	% of Daily Value
Calories	759	38%
Total Fat	46 g	66%
Saturated Fat	20.9 g	104%
Polyunsaturated Fat	5.3 g	—
Monounsaturated Fat	15.82 g	—
Trans Fat	0.41 g	—
Cholesterol	335 mg	112%
Sodium	2602 mg	130%
Total Carbohydrates	19.7 g	8%
Dietary Fiber	4.61 g	16%
Total Sugars	9.22 g	10%
Protein	66.3 g	133%
Vitamin A	597 mcg	75%
Vitamin C	19.54 mg	24%
Vitamin D	0.92 mcg	18%
Potassium	1886 mg	54%
Calcium	842 mg	105%
Iron	5.01 mg	36%

Lemon Garlic Roast Chicken

Prep time: 20 minutes
Cook time: 1 hour and 30 minutes
Total time: 1 hour 50 minutes

LEVEL 3: MODERATE

· ·

Roasting a chicken is easier than you think. Buying a fresh one from the grocery store will put you one hour away from roasted chicken excellence that pairs with any side dish you have on hand. This is a great recipe to build your cooking skills!

· ·

MAKES 7 SERVINGS

1 (6-pound) whole **chicken**, **giblets** and neck removed
Salt, to season
Cracked **black pepper**, to season
3 whole **lemons**, one cut in half, the others cut in quarters
2 whole **garlic heads**, cut in half
2 tablespoons dried **thyme**
2 tablespoons **butter**, melted
½ pound **bacon**

1. Preheat the oven to 425°F.

2. Pat the chicken dry and place in a roasting pan. Season inside the chicken cavity with the salt and pepper, then insert 2 lemon halves and 2 garlic head halves inside the cavity. Sprinkle outside and inside with thyme. Brush the melted butter all over the outside of the chicken and season with salt and pepper. Place the lemon quarters and remaining garlic head halves around the chicken in the roasting pan. Drape the bacon slices over the chicken.

3. Roast for 1 hour, then remove the bacon and set it aside. Continue to bake the chicken another 30 minutes, or until it reaches an internal temperature of 165°F.

4. Let the chicken rest for 10 minutes before carving. Serve on a platter with the bacon and roasted garlic and lemons.

NUTRITION	Per Serving	% of Daily Value
Calories	729	36%
Total Fat	55 g	78%
Saturated Fat	17.7 g	88%
Polyunsaturated Fat	2.27 g	—
Monounsaturated Fat	6.58 g	—
Trans Fat	0.04 g	—
Cholesterol	223 mg	74%
Sodium	509 mg	25%
Total Carbohydrates	6.02 g	2%
Dietary Fiber	1.28 g	5%
Total Sugars	0.82 g	1%
Protein	53 g	105%
Vitamin A	53 mcg	7%
Vitamin C	11.5 mg	14%
Vitamin D	0.13 mcg	3%
Potassium	615 mg	18%
Calcium	84 mg	11%
Iron	4.77 mg	34%

SNACKS

Cinnamon and Honey Yogurt Bowl

Prep time: 5 minutes
Cook time: 0 minutes
Total time: 5 minutes

LEVEL 1: VERY EASY

. . . .

Sometimes breaking a fast with a full meal is too heavy on the stomach. That's why I love to start my day with an energizing Greek yogurt bowl. This recipe brings together warm cinnamon, sweet honey, and crunchy almonds, creating a satisfying and protein-packed snack.

. . . .

MAKES 2 SERVINGS

1 cup fat-free plain **Greek yogurt**
1 teaspoon ground **cinnamon**
1 tablespoon **almonds**, chopped
1 teaspoon **honey**

1. Whisk the Greek yogurt and cinnamon together in a bowl, then divide the mixture between two small serving bowls.

2. Top each serving with the almonds and drizzle the honey over the top. Serve and enjoy!

NUTRITION	Per Serving	% of Daily Value
Calories	100	—
Total Fat	2.5 g	3%
Saturated Fat	0.2 g	1%
Polyunsaturated Fat	—	—
Monounsaturated Fat	0.2 g	—
Trans Fat	0.006 g	—
Cholesterol	5 mg	2%
Sodium	50 mg	2%
Total Carbohydrates	8 g	3%
Dietary Fiber	1 g	4%
Total Sugars	6 g	—
Protein	14 g	28%
Vitamin A	21.8 mcg	2%
Vitamin C	4 mcg	—
Vitamin D	—	—
Potassium	168 mg	4%
Calcium	140 mg	10%
Iron	0.2 mg	2%

Sesame Breadsticks

Prep time: 1 hour 45 minutes
Cook time: 20 minutes
Total time: 2 hours 5 minutes

LEVEL 5: AMBITIOUS

. . . .

I've been making these sesame breadsticks for years now. They pair well with any food and make a convenient snack when you're in a rush. Since they keep well for weeks if refrigerated, you can always make them in large batches to keep on hand!

. . . .

MAKES 8 SERVINGS

2 teaspoons granulated sugar
1½ teaspoons active dry yeast
1½ cups warm water
½ cup room-temperature water
4 cups whole-wheat flour
1 teaspoon salt
¼ cup extra-virgin olive oil
½ cup raw sesame seeds

1. Whisk the sugar, yeast, warm water, and room temperature water together in a bowl and set aside for 10 minutes.

2. Whisk together the flour and salt in a separate large bowl, then add the yeast mixture and the olive oil. Knead the dough for 15 minutes, until combined and smooth.

3. Place the dough in an oiled bowl and cover it with a clean kitchen towel. Move it to a warm area and allow it to rest for 1 hour, until doubled in size.

4. Preheat the oven to 490°F and line a baking sheet with parchment paper.

5. Divide the dough into ten even portions. Roll out each portion of dough into a long rope approximately ½ inch thick.

6. Place the ropes of dough onto the prepared baking sheet, twisting them into rings. Brush the breadsticks with water and sprinkle the sesame seeds on top.

7. Set the baking sheet aside for 20 minutes to allow the dough to rise, then bake for 15–20 minutes, until the breadsticks are golden and puffy. Remove from the oven and allow to cool on the pan for 5 minutes.

8. Place the breadsticks on a serving platter along with olive oil, butter, cheese, or jam, if desired. Refrigerate leftovers in an airtight container for up to 2 weeks.

NUTRITION	Per Serving	% of Daily Value
Calories	330	—
Total Fat	14 g	18%
Saturated Fat	2.4 g	12%
Polyunsaturated Fat	3.8 g	—
Monounsaturated Fat	7.3 g	—
Trans Fat	0.006 g	—
Cholesterol	—	—
Sodium	300 mg	13%
Total Carbohydrates	46 g	17%
Dietary Fiber	8 g	29%
Total Sugars	1 g	—
Protein	10 g	20%
Vitamin A	0.5 mcg	—
Vitamin C	4 mg	—
Vitamin D	—	—
Potassium	260 mg	6%
Calcium	31 mg	2%
Iron	2.8 mg	15%

Berry and Sunflower Yogurt Bowl

Prep time: 10 minutes
Cook time: 0 minutes
Total time: 10 minutes

LEVEL 1: VERY EASY

. . . .

This simple snack contains Ingredients that can boost your immunity, protect your heart health, and strengthen your metabolism. Sound too good to be true? The superfood combination of berries and sunflower seeds also makes this recipe as delicious as it is healthy!

. . . .

MAKES 1 SERVING

1 cup fat-free plain **Greek yogurt**
1 teaspoon **maple syrup**
1 tablespoon **sunflower seeds**
½ cup fresh mixed **berries**

1. Combine the Greek yogurt and maple syrup in a small bowl and stir to mix.

2. Add the mixture to a serving bowls. Top with ½ tablespoon sunflower seeds and ¼ cup mixed berries. Serve and enjoy!

NUTRITION	Per Serving	% of Daily Value
Calories	250	—
Total Fat	5 g	6%
Saturated Fat	0.8 g	4%
Polyunsaturated Fat	2.1 g	—
Monounsaturated Fat	1.7 g	—
Trans Fat	0.016 g	—
Cholesterol	—	—
Sodium	85 mg	4%
Total Carbohydrates	30 g	11%
Dietary Fiber	3 g	11%
Total Sugars	25 g	—
Protein	23 g	46%
Vitamin A	0.5 mcg	—
Vitamin C	3 mcg	—
Vitamin D	—	—
Potassium	476 mg	10%
Calcium	266 mg	20%
Iron	0.8 mg	4%

Lebanese Roasted Chickpeas

Prep time: 10 minutes
Cook time: 30 minutes
Total time: 45 minutes

LEVEL 3: MODERATE

. . . .

*Seasoned with citrusy sumac,
nutty cumin, and savory garlic
powder, these Lebanese-inspired
Roasted Chickpeas make a
flavorful snack. If you're a chip
person but would prefer to
snack on something a bit lighter,
this recipe will become your new
favorite!*

. . . .

MAKES 6 SERVINGS

2 (15-ounce) cans chickpeas,
    drained, rinsed, and peeled
¼ cup grated rennet-free
    Parmesan cheese
2 tablespoons extra-virgin olive oil
1 tablespoon lemon juice
2 teaspoons ground sumac
1 teaspoon ground cumin
1 teaspoon garlic powder
1 teaspoon cayenne pepper
1 teaspoon dried oregano
½ teaspoon black pepper

1. Preheat the oven to 475°F and line a rimmed baking sheet with parchment paper.

2. Dry the chickpeas using a kitchen towel and set them aside.

3. Whisk together the Parmesan, olive oil, lemon juice, sumac, cumin, garlic powder, cayenne, oregano, and pepper in a large bowl.

4. Add the chickpeas to the olive oil spice mixture, tossing to combine.

5. Spread the chickpeas out onto the prepared baking sheet and bake for 15 minutes, then turn the chickpeas over and bake for 10–15 minutes more, until they are light and crispy.

6. Remove from the oven and let cool for 5 minutes. Serve warm or at room temperature. Refrigerate leftovers in an airtight container for up to 5 days.

NUTRITION	Per Serving	% of Daily Value
Calories	180	—
Total Fat	8 g	10%
Saturated Fat	1.4 g	7%
Polyunsaturated Fat	1.3 g	—
Monounsaturated Fat	4 g	—
Trans Fat	0.039 g	—
Cholesterol	5 mg	2%
Sodium	260 mg	11%
Total Carbohydrates	21 g	8%
Dietary Fiber	6 g	21%
Total Sugars	4 g	—
Protein	7 g	14%
Vitamin A	62 mcg	6%
Vitamin C	3.8 mg	6%
Vitamin D	0.025 mcg	—
Potassium	126 mg	2%
Calcium	80 mg	6%
Iron	1.2 mg	6%

Berry Jam and Goat Cheese Crostini

Prep time: 5 minutes
Cook time: 0 minutes
Total time: 5 minutes

LEVEL 1: VERY EASY

. . . .

*Nothing pairs more perfectly
with salty cheese than a berry
spread. This recipe calls for
mixed berry jam, but feel free
to use whatever berry jam you
have at home. Topped with fresh
spearmint leaves, this simple
and elegant dish is guaranteed
to win the hearts of your guests.*

. . . .

MAKES 1 SERVING

3 tablespoons goat cheese
2 slices whole-wheat bread,
   toasted
3 tablespoons sugar-free mixed
   berry jam
¼ cup tightly packed fresh
   spearmint leaves

1. Spread the goat cheese onto each slice of toasted bread.

2. Spread the mixed berry jam over the goat cheese and garnish the crostini with the spearmint leaves. Serve and enjoy!

NUTRITION	Per Serving	% of Daily Value
Calories	480	—
Total Fat	21 g	27%
Saturated Fat	12.53 g	63%
Polyunsaturated Fat	2.134 g	—
Monounsaturated Fat	1.505 g	—
Trans Fat	21 g	—
Cholesterol	45 mg	15%
Sodium	300 mg	13%
Total Carbohydrates	55 g	20%
Dietary Fiber	6 g	21%
Total Sugars	21 g	—
Protein	19 g	38%
Vitamin A	260 mcg	16%
Vitamin C	17.5 mcg	29%
Vitamin D	0.5 mcg	—
Potassium	422 mg	8%
Calcium	231 mg	20%
Iron	4.99 mg	30%

Dried Fig and
Nut Yogurt Bowl

Prep time: 5 minutes
Cook time: 0 minutes
Total time: 5 minutes

LEVEL 1: VERY EASY

. . . .

*Greek yogurt has to be one of
the most satisfying foods on
the planet! It's rich in protein,
making you feel fuller for longer.
Here it's topped with comforting
cinnamon, earthy walnuts,
and sweet figs, elevating your
typical yogurt bowl into a
Mediterranean treat.*

. . . .

MAKES 2 SERVINGS

1 cup fat-free plain **Greek yogurt**
1 teaspoon ground **cinnamon**
¼ cup halved dried **figs**
1 tablespoon **walnuts**, chopped
1 teaspoon **honey**

1. Whisk together the Greek yogurt and cinnamon in a bowl.

2. Divide the mixture between two serving bowls and top each portion with the figs, walnuts, and a drizzle of honey. Serve and enjoy!

NUTRITION	Per Serving	% of Daily Value
Calories	150	—
Total Fat	2.5 g	3%
Saturated Fat	0.3 g	2%
Polyunsaturated Fat	1.4 g	—
Monounsaturated Fat	006 g	—
Trans Fat	0.008 g	—
Cholesterol	—	—
Sodium	40 mg	—
Total Carbohydrates	22 g	8%
Dietary Fiber	2 g	7%
Total Sugars	18 g	—
Protein	12 g	24%
Vitamin A	1.3 mcg	—
Vitamin C	5 mg	—
Vitamin D	—	—
Potassium	261 mg	6%
Calcium	156 mg	10%
Iron	0.5 mg	4%

Avocado Hummus with Cucumber

Prep time: 10 minutes
Cook time: 0 minutes
Total time: 10 minutes

LEVEL 2: EASY

. . . .

Picture it—guacamole and hummus blended into one ingenious dip. This simple recipe makes the creamiest hummus you've ever tasted, and the flavor is simply unbelievable. Here it's served with fresh cucumber slices, but feel free to experiment with other pairings—your imagination is the only limit.

. . . .

MAKES 1 SERVING

1 (15-ounce) can chickpeas, drained, + 2 tablespoons chickpea liquid drained from the can
1 ripe avocado, sliced
¼ cup tahini
1 garlic clove
1 teaspoon ground cumin
½ teaspoon salt
¼ cup lemon juice
1 tablespoon extra-virgin olive oil
5 medium cucumbers, sliced

1. Combine the chickpeas, chickpea liquid, avocado, tahini, garlic, cumin, salt, lemon juice, and olive oil in a blender. Purée until the hummus is very smooth.

2. Transfer the hummus to a serving bowl. Arrange the cucumber slices on a serving platter and serve alongside the hummus.

NUTRITION	Per Serving	% of Daily Value
Calories	300	—
Total Fat	21 g	27%
Saturated Fat	2.8 g	14%
Polyunsaturated Fat	5.4 g	—
Monounsaturated Fat	1.8 g	—
Trans Fat	0.002 g	—
Cholesterol	—	—
Sodium	480 mg	21%
Total Carbohydrates	24 g	9%
Dietary Fiber	9 g	32%
Total Sugars	3 g	—
Protein	8 g	16%
Vitamin A	43 mcg	4%
Vitamin C	1.6 mg	2%
Vitamin D	—	—
Potassium	431 mg	10%
Calcium	108 mg	8%
Iron	2.7 mg	15%

Greek Yogurt Bowl with Muesli

Prep time: 5 minutes
Cook time: 0 minutes
Total time: 5 minutes

LEVEL 1: VERY EASY

. . . .

Greek yogurt bowls are a favorite in my family. They're simple and quick, but also delicious and loaded with health benefits. While muesli usually contains its own nuts and fruits, I like to add even more, enhancing the yum factor. Sprinkled with cinnamon and drizzled with honey, this recipe is perfect for busy days.

. . . .

MAKES 1 SERVING

⅔ cup plain **Greek yogurt**

½ cup sugar-free, gluten-free muesli

1 tablespoon chopped dried apricots

1 tablespoon chopped **walnuts**

1 tablespoon chopped **almonds**

½ teaspoon ground **cinnamon**

1 tablespoon raw **honey**

1. Place the Greek yogurt in a serving bowl and top with the muesli, apricots, walnuts, almonds, and cinnamon.

2. Drizzle the honey over the top and serve.

NUTRITION	Per Serving	% of Daily Value
Calories	430	—
Total Fat	19 g	24%
Saturated Fat	5 g	25%
Polyunsaturated Fat	3.595 g	—
Monounsaturated Fat	4.217 g	—
Trans Fat	0.001 g	—
Cholesterol	20 mg	7%
Sodium	80 mg	3%
Total Carbohydrates	53 g	19%
Dietary Fiber	5 g	18%
Total Sugars	37 g	—
Protein	13 g	26%
Vitamin A	33 mcg	47%
Vitamin C	1.8 mcg	3%
Vitamin D	0.025 mcg	1%
Potassium	493 mg	12%
Calcium	238 mg	25%
Iron	1.21 mg	7%

Greek Pasteli

Prep time: 5 minutes
Cook time: 5 minutes
Total time: 2 hours 10 minutes

LEVEL 4: CHALLENGING

. . . .

If you love a sweet snack but prefer healthy options, this treat is for you! In Greece, pasteli is traditionally offered to both the bride and groom on their wedding day, as the sesame seeds symbolize fertility and the honey represents a sweet life. Known as the world's first energy bar, pasteli was invented to fuel the original Olympians.

. . . .

MAKES 10 SERVINGS

½ cup **maltitol syrup**
1 cup **sesame seeds**
½ cup **sunflower seeds**

1. Lay out two large sheets of parchment paper on the counter and coat them with nonstick cooking spray.

2. Place the maltitol syrup in a saucepan over medium-high heat and bring it to a boil.

3. Stir in the sesame seeds and sunflower seeds, then immediately pour the mixture onto one of the parchment paper sheets.

4. Top the mixture with the other sheet of parchment paper and flatten it to a ½-inch thickness with a rolling pin.

5. Carefully peel off the top piece of parchment paper and allow the pasteli to cool for 15 minutes.

6. Cut into 10 even-sized bars using a sharp knife or a pizza cutter.

7. Refrigerate the bars for at least 2 hours before serving. Refrigerate leftovers in an airtight container for up to 5 days

NUTRITION	Per Serving	% of Daily Value
Calories	140	—
Total Fat	12 g	15%
Saturated Fat	1.5 g	8%
Polyunsaturated Fat	5 g	—
Monounsaturated Fat	4.5 g	—
Trans Fat	—	—
Cholesterol	—	—
Sodium	25 mg	1%
Total Carbohydrates	7 g	3%
Dietary Fiber	2 g	7%
Total Sugars	3 g	—
Protein	4 g	8%
Vitamin A	0.3 mcg	—
Vitamin C	2.4 mg	4%
Vitamin D	—	—
Potassium	95 mg	2%
Calcium	15 mg	2%
Iron	1.2 mg	6%

Almond and Walnut Bars

Prep time: 5 minutes
Cook time: 5 minutes
Total time: 2 hours 25 minutes

LEVEL 4: CHALLENGING

. . . .

Nuts are incorporated into countless Mediterranean dishes, both sweet and savory! These nut bars are seasoned with a hint of cinnamon and favor the sweeter side of life. Thanks to the health benefits of nuts, these bars can help lower your "bad" cholesterol levels, reduce inflammation, and improve your digestion.

. . . .

MAKES 10 SERVINGS

½ cup **maltitol syrup**
1 cup raw and whole **almonds**
½ cup raw and whole **walnuts**
1 teaspoon ground **cinnamon**

1. Lay out two large sheets of parchment paper on the counter and coat them with nonstick cooking spray.

2. Place the maltitol syrup in a saucepan over medium-high heat and bring it to a boil.

3. Stir in the almonds, walnuts, and cinnamon, then immediately pour the mixture onto one of the parchment paper sheets.

4. Top the mixture with the other sheet of parchment paper and flatten it to a ½-inch thickness with a rolling pin.

5. Carefully peel off the top piece of parchment paper and allow the bars to cool for 15 minutes.

6. Cut into 10 even-sized bars using a sharp knife or a pizza cutter.

7. Refrigerate the bars for at least 2 hours before serving. Refrigerate leftovers in an airtight container for up to 5 days.

NUTRITION	Per Serving	% of Daily Value
Calories	140	—
Total Fat	11 g	14%
Saturated Fat	0.9 g	5%
Polyunsaturated Fat	4.5 g	—
Monounsaturated Fat	5 g	—
Trans Fat	0.002 g	—
Cholesterol	—	—
Sodium	20 mg	1%
Total Carbohydrates	9 g	3%
Dietary Fiber	2 g	7%
Total Sugars	5 g	—
Protein	4 g	8%
Vitamin A	0.4 mcg	—
Vitamin C	3.8 mg	6%
Vitamin D	—	—
Potassium	6204 mg	130%
Calcium	624 mg	50%
Iron	0.1 mg	—

Classic Italian Bruschetta

Prep time: 2 hours 10 minutes
Cook time: 25 minutes
Total time: 2 hours 35 minutes

LEVEL 3: MODERATE

. . . .

Bruschetta is always a crowd-pleaser. This speedy recipe will leave your loved ones thinking you spent all day in the kitchen! The secret to perfect bruschetta is the bread; be sure to pick a crunchy, crusty loaf that the tomato mixture can soften with its delectable juices.

. . . .

MAKES 4 SERVINGS

1½ cups chopped ripe tomatoes
1 teaspoon salt
5 tablespoons extra-virgin olive oil
2 large garlic cloves, minced
8 large basil leaves, chopped
1 teaspoon black pepper
4 slices crusty whole-wheat
    bread, toasted

1. Place the tomatoes in a colander and place the colander into the sink.

2. Stir in the salt and allow the tomatoes to rest for 1–2 hours.

3. Combine the olive oil and garlic in a saucepan over medium-low heat and cook for 2–3 minutes or until the garlic softens and becomes fragrant. Set aside to cool.

4. Combine the garlic oil, tomatoes, basil, and pepper in a medium bowl.

5. Arrange the bread slices on a serving plate and top with the tomato mixture. Serve and enjoy!

NUTRITION	Per Serving	% of Daily Value
Calories	260	—
Total Fat	19 g	24%
Saturated Fat	2.6 g	13%
Polyunsaturated Fat	2.8 g	—
Monounsaturated Fat	12 g	—
Trans Fat	0.008 g	—
Cholesterol	—	—
Sodium	700 mg	30%
Total Carbohydrates	26 g	6%
Dietary Fiber	4 g	14%
Total Sugars	4 g	—
Protein	4 g	8%
Vitamin A	211 mcg	120%
Vitamin C	12 g	20%
Vitamin D	—	—
Potassium	390 mg	8%
Calcium	390 mg	30%
Iron	0.2 mg	2%

Zucchini Latkes

Prep time: 20 minutes
Cook time: 25 minutes
Total time: 45 minutes

LEVEL 3: MODERATE

. . . .

*Some recipes just have to be
tasted to really appreciate their
flavor, and this is one of them.
Make sure to drain the zucchini
well so that your latkes fry up
crisp. These are a delicious
alternative to traditional potato
latkes, ensuring you meet your
keto guidelines.*

. . . .

MAKES 4 SERVINGS

2 medium **zucchini**, grated
⅓ cup **Parmesan cheese**, grated
2 tablespoons finely ground
   almond flour
2 large **eggs**
2 tablespoons **olive oil**
Salt, to taste
Cracked **black pepper**, to taste
½ cup low-fat **sour cream**,
   for serving

1. Drain and squeeze the shredded zucchini to remove excess moisture. Place in a bowl and combine with the cheese, flour, and eggs. Mix thoroughly, then let rest for 3 minutes.

2. Heat the oil in a frying pan over medium heat. When hot, drop ¼ cup of the zucchini mixture into the frying pan for each latke, working in batches if necessary. Use a wooden spoon to shape latkes into rounds. Cook for 2–3 minutes, then turn latkes over gently and fry for 2–3 minutes more on the other side. Set aside on a paper towel-lined plate while you repeat with the remaining batches.

3. Season latkes with salt and pepper to taste, and serve with a dollop of sour cream.

NUTRITION	Per Serving	% of Daily Value
Calories	158	8%
Total Fat	13 g	19%
Saturated Fat	2.95 g	15%
Polyunsaturated Fat	1.73 g	—
Monounsaturated Fat	7.6 g	—
Trans Fat	0.01 g	—
Cholesterol	97.5	33%
Sodium	121 mg	6%
Total Carbohydrates	4 g	2%
Dietary Fiber	1.31 g	5%
Total Sugars	2.56 g	3%
Protein	7.3 g	15%
Vitamin A	112 mcg	14%
Vitamin C	17 g	21%
Vitamin D	0.54 mcg	11%
Potassium	304 mg	9%
Calcium	115 mg	14%
Iron	0.98 mg	7%

Zoodle Caprese

Prep time: 20 minutes
Cook time: 20 minutes
Total time: 40 minutes

LEVEL 3: MODERATE

· ·

Even though this is a Diabetes cookbook, we wanted to ensure we included a recipe that incorporates zoodles—it's a keto staple and just such an amazing method to learn! The trend of spiralizing veggies is a dieter's dream come true. Any hard summer or winter squash will work well in a spiralizer, and you can find a handy spiralizing gadget at almost any grocery store.

· ·

MAKES 4 SERVINGS

4 large zucchini, spiralized or shredded lengthwise with a mandolin
2 tablespoons olive oil
Salt, to taste
Cracked black pepper, to taste
2 cups halved cherry tomatoes
1 cup small fresh mozzarella balls
¼ cup fresh basil leaves
2 tablespoons balsamic vinegar

1. Toss the zucchini noodles with the olive oil in a large bowl. Add salt and pepper to taste, then set aside to marinate for 15 minutes.

2. Add the tomatoes, mozzarella, and basil to the zucchini and stir gently to incorporate. Drizzle the vinegar over the top and serve.

NUTRITION	Per Serving	% of Daily Value
Calories	208	10%
Total Fat	13 g	18%
Saturated Fat	4.1 g	21%
Polyunsaturated Fat	1.23 g	—
Monounsaturated Fat	6.52 g	—
Trans Fat	—	—
Cholesterol	18 g	6%
Sodium	398 mg	20%
Total Carbohydrates	15 g	6%
Dietary Fiber	4 g	14%
Total Sugars	11 g	12%
Protein	11 g	23%
Vitamin A	435 mcg	54%
Vitamin C	65.4 g	82%
Vitamin D	0.08 mcg	2%
Potassium	267 mg	38%
Calcium	282 mg	35%
Iron	1.57 mg	11%

Mixed Roasted Vegetables

Prep time: 15 minutes
Cook time: 30 minutes
Total time: 45 minutes

LEVEL 3: MODERATE

. . . .

Use this recipe to spotlight your local farmers' market bounty. The vegetable dressing goes well with a wide variety of veggies, so find your favorite combo from the list of suggestions below. To mix things up even more, you can also swap out the Italian seasoning used here for your own favorite blends.

. . . .

MAKES 8 SERVINGS

For the dressing
¼ cup **olive oil**
2 tablespoons **balsamic vinegar**
1 tablespoon minced **garlic**
1 teaspoon **Italian seasoning**
Salt, to taste
Cracked **black pepper**, to taste

Vegetables
10 cups chopped mixed vegetables, cut into 1½-inch pieces, any combination of the following:
· Broccoli florets
· Cauliflower florets
· Zucchini
· Bell peppers
· Onions
· Mushrooms
· Eggplant
· Cabbage

1. Preheat the oven to 425°F.

2. Whisk all the dressing Ingredients together in a small bowl.

3. Place the chopped mixed vegetables in a large bowl, pour dressing over the veggies, and toss to coat.

4. Divide the vegetables between two oiled baking sheets and spread out in a single layer. Roast for 30 minutes, or until golden brown. Let sit for 3 minutes, then serve.

(does not include vegetable nutritional information as it will vary depending on the recipe)

NUTRITION	Per Serving	% of Daily Value
Calories	68	3%
Total Fat	7 g	10%
Saturated Fat	0.98 g	5%
Polyunsaturated Fat	0.75 g	—
Monounsaturated Fat	5.2 g	—
Trans Fat	—	—
Cholesterol	—	—
Sodium	1.24 mg	—
Total Carbohydrates	1 g	—
Dietary Fiber	—	—
Total Sugars	0.61 g	1%
Protein	—	—
Vitamin A	—	—
Vitamin C	0.33 g	—
Vitamin D	—	—
Potassium	8.79 mg	—
Calcium	3.07 mg	—
Iron	0.09 mg	11%

DESSERTS

Chocolate Hummus

Prep time: 11 minutes
Cook time: 0 minutes
Total time: 11 minutes

LEVEL 2: EASY

. . . .

Hummus isn't just an appetizer . . . it can be a dessert too! This Chocolate Hummus is the perfect light dessert, bringing any meal to a satisfying close. It's creamy and fluffy, and best served with pita or cinnamon-sugar tortilla chips. As with other Mediterranean desserts, this hummus is a rich source of vitamins and minerals, improving digestion and aiding in weight management.

. . . .

MAKES 4 SERVINGS

1 (15-ounce) can chickpeas, rinsed and drained
¼ cup cocoa powder
4 tablespoons maple syrup
1 teaspoon cinnamon
1 teaspoon vanilla extract
Zest of 1 lemon
1–2 tablespoons water

1. Combine the chickpeas, cocoa powder, maple syrup, cinnamon, vanilla extract, and lemon zest in a blender or food processor and purée until slightly smooth.

2. Add the water, 1 tablespoon at a time, and continue to purée until the hummus reaches the desired consistency.

3. Spoon into a serving dish and serve! Refrigerate leftovers in an airtight container for up to 3 days.

NUTRITION	Per Serving	% of Daily Value
Calories	220	10%
Total Fat	4.2 g	4.5%
Saturated Fat	0.54 g	3%
Polyunsaturated Fat	1.06 g	—
Monounsaturated Fat	0.76 g	—
Trans Fat	—	—
Cholesterol	—	—
Sodium	267 mg	18%
Total Carbohydrates	42.69 g	17%
Dietary Fiber	8.9 g	36%
Total Sugars	17.33 g	—
Protein	8.65 g	16%
Vitamin A	27 mcg	1%
Vitamin C	4.8 mcg	6%
Vitamin D	—	—
Potassium	331 mg	7%
Calcium	82 mg	8%
Iron	2.09 mg	12%

Pistachio Ice Cream

Prep time: 30 minutes
Cook time: 0 minutes
Total time: 7 hours 30 minutes

LEVEL 1: VERY EASY

. . . .

*Crafted with both roasted
pistachios and pistachio butter,
this dairy-free ice cream is
absolutely irresistible, and I
assure you, one scoop will never
be enough! So eat up, because
this is one dessert that keeps
your blood sugar, cholesterol,
and blood pressure in check.*

. . . .

MAKES 6 SERVINGS

2 cups **unsweetened almond milk**
½ cup **pistachio butter**
⅓ cup **granulated sugar**
1 teaspoon **vanilla extract**
¼ teaspoon **salt**
¾ cup **unsalted pistachios,**
    roasted and chopped

1. In a mixing bowl, whisk all the Ingredients together, except for the chopped pistachios. Blend well.*

2. Transfer mixture to an airtight freezer-safe container with a lid, cover and freeze for 2 hours.

3. Remove from freezer and stir again. Refreeze mixture for another 2 hours.

4. Uncover mixture and add the chopped pistachios, stirring one last time. Cover and return to freezer for another 3–4 hours, or until firm.

5. Once desired consistency is reached, serve in small dessert bowls.

***Note:** If using an ice cream maker, place blended mixture in ice cream maker and follow manufacturer's directions.*

NUTRITION	Per Serving	% of Daily Value
Calories	218	10%
Total Fat	14.21 g	29%
Saturated Fat	2.926 g	—
Polyunsaturated Fat	3.636 g	—
Monounsaturated Fat	6.744 g	—
Trans Fat	—	—
Cholesterol	8 mg	—
Sodium	133 mg	9%
Total Carbohydrates	16.8 g	7%
Dietary Fiber	2.6 g	10%
Total Sugars	11.55 g	—
Protein	7.86 g	14%
Vitamin A	214 mcg	9%
Vitamin C	1 mcg	1%
Vitamin D	2 mcg	—
Potassium	368 mg	8%
Calcium	119 mg	12%
Iron	1.05mg	6%

Peach Apricot Sherbet

Prep time: 10 minutes
Cook time: 0 minutes
Total time: 5 hours 10 minutes

LEVEL 2: EASY

. . . .

Sherbet is ice cream's lighter cousin. Using only four simple Ingredients, this fruit-rich frozen treat takes on a beautiful pastel yellow color. With its tangy balance of sweet and tart, this recipe will rival your go-to ice cream.

. . . .

MAKES 6 SERVINGS

3 large peaches, peeled, pitted, and sliced

3 apricots, peeled, pitted, and sliced

1 (14-ounce) can sweetened condensed milk

1 teaspoon vanilla extract

1. Arrange the fruit slices in a single layer on a parchment-lined cookie sheet and freeze for 4–5 hours.

2. In a blender, combine the fruit, condensed milk, and vanilla. Process until smooth and creamy with the texture of soft serve.

3. Serve immediately. Freeze leftovers in an airtight container for up to 3 days.

NUTRITION	Per Serving	% of Daily Value
Calories	257	12%
Total Fat	6.05 g	12%
Saturated Fat	3.651 g	—
Polyunsaturated Fat	0.314 g	—
Monounsaturated Fat	1.964 g	—
Trans Fat	—	—
Cholesterol	22 mg	—
Sodium	86 mg	6%
Total Carbohydrates	46.84 g	19%
Dietary Fiber	1.7 g	7%
Total Sugars	45.32 g	—
Protein	6.34 g	12%
Vitamin A	799 mcg	34%
Vitamin C	9.3 mcg	12%
Vitamin D	4 mcg	1%
Potassium	460 mg	10%
Calcium	196 mg	20%
Iron	0.44 mg	2%

Mediterranean Crêpes

Prep time: 10 minutes
Cook time: 20 minutes
Total time: 1 hour

LEVEL 3: MODERATE

. . . .

We all know that crêpes are associated with French cuisine. However, these Mediterranean Crêpes are a fresh spin on the classic dish. Serve with fig or apricot preserves, freshly whipped cream, jam, or fresh fruits to maximize flavor—and health benefits!

. . . .

MAKES 4 SERVINGS

4 cups milk
2½ cups all-purpose flour
4 large eggs
1 teaspoon sunflower oil
¼ teaspoon salt
1 teaspoon unsalted butter

1. Combine all the Ingredients, except butter, in a blender and process until smooth.

2. Let the crêpe batter rest for 30 minutes at room temperature.

3. Set a small (7½-inch) frying pan over medium-high heat. Once hot, add the butter,* swirling it around the pan to melt.

4. Use a small ladle to scoop enough of the crêpe batter to coat the entire bottom of the pan. Swirl the pan to spread the batter or use the bottom of the ladle.

5. Cook until the crêpe batter dries completely and the edges pull away from the pan.

6. With a spatula, flip the crêpe over and cook an additional 1–2 minutes, or until golden brown. Transfer each cooked crêpe to a parchment-lined cookie sheet, spread apart so they don't stick together.

7. Fill the crêpes with your favorite fillings: whipped cream, preserved fruits, or nut butter. Serve and enjoy!

*Note: The first crêpe will likely absorb most of the butter, which makes it oilier than the rest. The remaining crêpes will cook perfectly.

NUTRITION	Per Serving	% of Daily Value
Calories	484	23%
Total Fat	12.12 g	25%
Saturated Fat	5.265 g	—
Polyunsaturated Fat	1.523 g	—
Monounsaturated Fat	4.392 g	—
Trans Fat	0.226 g	—
Cholesterol	207 mg	—
Sodium	333 mg	22%
Total Carbohydrates	71.69 g	29%
Dietary Fiber	2.1 g	8%
Total Sugars	12.74 g	—
Protein	22.44 g	41%
Vitamin A	754 mcg	32%
Vitamin C	0.5 mcg	1%
Vitamin D	161 mcg	27%
Potassium	465 mg	11%
Calcium	333 mg	33%
Iron	4.46 mg	25%

Spiced Walnut Fruitcake

Prep time: 30 minutes
Cook time: 55 minutes
Total time: 1 hour 35 minutes

LEVEL 3: MODERATE

. . . .

One bite of this and you will understand why fruitcakes have been popular since Roman times! This version is studded with Mediterranean favorites, including walnuts, coconut, and dates. The fragrant spices enhance the flavor and transform this dessert from a typical fruitcake to an extraordinary one—to be enjoyed year-round.

. . . .

MAKES 7 SERVINGS

1 cup brown rice flour

1 cup almond flour

½ cup monk fruit sweetener

2 teaspoons baking powder

1 teaspoon ground cinnamon

½ teaspoon ground nutmeg

½ teaspoon ground ginger

½ teaspoon ground cloves

½ teaspoon ground cardamom

¼ teaspoon sea salt

⅓ cup extra-virgin olive oil

2 large eggs

⅓ cup almond milk

1 teaspoon vanilla extract

1 teaspoon almond extract

1 cup chopped and roasted walnuts

½ cup unsweetened coconut flakes

½ cup pitted and chopped dates

1. Preheat oven to 350°F and coat a round 7-inch cake pan with nonstick cooking spray.

2. Whisk together the flours, monk fruit sweetener, baking powder, cinnamon, nutmeg, ginger, cloves, cardamom, and salt in a large bowl.

3. Whisk together the olive oil, eggs, almond milk, vanilla extract, and almond extract in a separate small bowl, until well combined.

4. Add the olive oil mixture to the dry Ingredients, stirring just until incorporated. Fold in the walnuts, coconut flakes, and dates.

5. Pour the batter into the prepared cake pan and bake for 35–55 minutes, until a skewer comes out clean.

6. Cool for 10 minutes in the pan, then remove to a wire rack to cool completely. Serve and enjoy! Refrigerate leftovers in an airtight container for up to 3 days.

NUTRITION	Per Serving	% of Daily Value
Calories	359	16%
Total Fat	22.18 g	46%
Saturated Fat	4.719 g	—
Polyunsaturated Fat	7.037 g	—
Monounsaturated Fat	9.515 g	—
Trans Fat	0.011 g	—
Cholesterol	55 mg	—
Sodium	140 mg	9%
Total Carbohydrates	35.29 g	14%
Dietary Fiber	3.6 g	14%
Total Sugars	10.69 g	—
Protein	6.93 g	13%
Vitamin A	178 mcg	8%
Vitamin C	0.4 mcg	1%
Vitamin D	12 mcg	2%
Potassium	430 mg	9%
Calcium	134 mg	13%
Iron	1.53 mg	9%

Date Almond Brownies

Prep time: 40 minutes
Cook time: 30 minutes
Total time: 1 hour 10 minutes

LEVEL 3: MODERATE

. . . .

You can always count on the caramel-like flavor of Medjool dates to add the perfect amount of sweetness to any recipe. Brimming with fiber and antioxidants, these brownies can improve digestion. The toasted almonds and shredded coconut paired with a touch of espresso powder make this dessert the definition of velvety goodness!

. . . .

MAKES 16 SERVINGS

½ cup **unsweetened shredded coconut**

½ cup **almonds**

1 cup pitted **Medjool dates**

¾ cup **hot water**

¾ cup **almond flour**

½ cup **unsweetened cocoa powder**

3 tablespoons **stevia**

1 tablespoon **vanilla extract**

1 teaspoon **espresso powder**

1 teaspoon **baking powder**

¼ teaspoon **sea salt**

1. Preheat the oven to 350°F and line a cookie sheet with parchment paper. Coat an 8-inch-square baking dish with nonstick cooking spray.

2. Evenly spread the shredded coconut and almonds in a single layer onto the prepared cookie sheet and bake 8–10 minutes, stirring every two minutes, until the coconut is golden. Set aside to cool completely.

3. Combine the dates and hot water in a small bowl for 10 minutes, allowing the dates to soften.

4. Drain the dates and transfer to a food processor, blending into a smooth paste.

5. Add the almond flour, cocoa powder, stevia, vanilla extract, espresso powder, baking powder, and salt to the food processor's bowl and blend well, scraping down the sides as needed, until a smooth batter is formed.

6. Remove lid and blade from the food processor and fold in the toasted almonds and coconut.

7. Pour batter into the prepared baking dish and bake for 18–20 minutes or until the center of the cake springs back when lightly touched.

8. Cool for 10 minutes in the pan, then transfer to a wire rack, cooling completely.

9. Cut into 16 squares and serve. Refrigerate leftovers in an airtight container for up to 3 days.

NUTRITION	Per Serving	% of Daily Value
Calories	101	5%
Total Fat	4.85 g	10%
Saturated Fat	0.561 g	—
Polyunsaturated Fat	1.112 g	—
Monounsaturated Fat	2.935 g	—
Trans Fat	0.001 g	—
Cholesterol	—	—
Sodium	68 mg	5%
Total Carbohydrates	19.89 g	8%
Dietary Fiber	2.9 g	12%
Total Sugars	10.16 g	—
Protein	2.69 g	5%
Vitamin A	21 mcg	1%
Vitamin C	0.2 mcg	—
Vitamin D	—	—
Potassium	252 mg	5%
Calcium	60 mg	6%
Iron	0.93 mg	5%

Olive Oil Chocolate Chip Cookies

Prep time: 35 minutes
Cook time: 12 minutes
Total time: 47 minutes

LEVEL 3: MODERATE

. . . .

Like most of us, you've probably baked more than your fair share of chocolate chip cookies and aren't keen to try another recipe. Before you pass this one by, I'm pretty sure it may well become your favorite. Substituting olive oil for butter gives these cookies a healthier edge, plus they are as perfect for dessert as they are for an afternoon pick-me-up.

. . . .

MAKES 24 COOKIES

2 cups **all-purpose flour**
1 teaspoon **sea salt**
½ teaspoon **baking soda**
1 cup **extra-virgin olive oil**
1 cup light **brown sugar**
½ cup **granulated sugar**
1 tablespoon **vanilla extract**
1 large **egg**
2 cups **semisweet chocolate chips**

1. Preheat oven to 350°F and line two cookie sheets with parchment paper.

2. Whisk together flour, salt, and baking soda in a small bowl and set aside.

3. Whisk together the olive oil, brown sugar, granulated sugar, and vanilla extract in a separate large bowl. Add the egg and whisk until smooth.

4. Add the dry Ingredients to the wet Ingredients in batches, stirring until well incorporated. Fold in the chocolate chips.

5. Roll the cookie dough into 24 balls (about 2 tablespoons each) and place on the prepared cookie sheets, leaving 2 inches of space between them. Slightly flatten each ball with the palm of your hand.

5. Bake both cookie sheets at the same time for 10–12 minutes, until the edges are golden brown.

6. Cool cookies on the pan for 5 minutes, then remove to a wire rack to cool completely. Serve and enjoy! Refrigerate leftovers in an airtight container for up to 3 days.

NUTRITION	Per Serving	% of Daily Value
Calories	226	10%
Total Fat	9.11 g	19%
Saturated Fat	3.552 g	—
Polyunsaturated Fat	0.47 g	—
Monounsaturated Fat	2.941 g	—
Trans Fat	0.009 g	—
Cholesterol	12 mg	—
Sodium	207 mg	14%
Total Carbohydrates	33.66 g	14%
Dietary Fiber	1.5 g	6%
Total Sugars	23.19 g	—
Protein	2.22 g	4%
Vitamin A	32 mcg	1%
Vitamin C	—	—
Vitamin D	2 mcg	—
Potassium	30 mg	1%
Calcium	17 mg	2%
Iron	1.14 mg	6%

Blueberry Yogurt with Chickpea Topping

Prep time: 15 minutes

Cook time: 12 minutes

Total time: 4 hours 27 minutes

LEVEL 2: EASY

. . . .

Whoever said chickpeas should be reserved for dinner recipes hasn't tried this tempting dessert! If you've never caramelized chickpeas, brace yourself, as they make an excellent dessert topping. This light treat is a great ending to a heavy meal and is also perfect for breakfast.

. . . .

MAKES 2 SERVINGS

2 cups **blueberries**

3 tablespoons **honey**

1 teaspoon dried **lavender**

Zest of 1 **lemon**

Juice of 1 **lemon**

2 cups plain **Greek yogurt**

2 teaspoons **unsalted butter**

½ cup **chickpeas**, boiled and peeled

2 tablespoons **granulated sugar**

1. Choose two (8-ounce) containers; these can be jars or bowls, glass, or plastic.*

2. Add the blueberries, honey, lavender, lemon zest, and lemon juice to a blender and process until well combined.

3. Pour into a medium bowl and add the yogurt, stirring briefly and only until streaks of the blueberry mixture are visible, giving a marbleized appearance. Set aside.

4. Melt the butter in a skillet set over medium-high heat.

5. Add the chickpeas and sugar and cook for 5 minutes, until the sugar melts and the chickpeas are caramelized.

6. Turn the chickpeas onto a silicone baking mat in a single layer and allow to cool completely.

7. Divide the yogurt mixture between the two containers and top with the caramelized chickpeas.

8. Wrap with plastic wrap or place the lid on your containers and refrigerate for 3–4 hours. Serve and enjoy!

*Note: Choose containers with well-fitting lids for an on-the-go breakfast, lunch, or snack.

NUTRITION	Per Serving	% of Daily Value
Calories	492	23%
Total Fat	13.49 g	25%
Saturated Fat	7.738 g	—
Polyunsaturated Fat	1.068 g	—
Monounsaturated Fat	3.497 g	—
Trans Fat	0.156 g	—
Cholesterol	42 mg	—
Sodium	150 mg	10%
Total Carbohydrates	84.96 g	38%
Dietary Fiber	7.1 g	28%
Total Sugars	67.47 g	—
Protein	13.49 g	25%
Vitamin A	455 mcg	20%
Vitamin C	29.4 mcg	39%
Vitamin D	8 mcg	1%
Potassium	663 mg	14%
Calcium	334 mg	33%
Iron	1.91 mg	11%

Graham Cracker Coriander Yogurt Cups

Prep time: 20 minutes
Cook time: 0 minutes
Total time: 20 min + overnight

LEVEL 2: EASY

. . . .

Coriander has been used in Egyptian culture as medicine and as a cooking spice since 1550 BC. This dessert features creamy yogurt and a cream cheese filling with a graham cracker and coriander crust. Garnish with fresh mint, honey, and berries and enjoy as dessert or any time of the day!

. . . .

MAKES 3 SERVINGS

For the crust
¾ cup **graham cracker crumbs**
½ cup **unsalted butter**, melted
¼ cup **granola**
¼ cup **brown sugar**
½ tablespoons **poppy seeds**
1 teaspoon ground **coriander**

For the filling
1 cup **cream cheese**, softened
½ cup **Greek yogurt**
1 teaspoon **vanilla extract**

For the topping
½ cup diced fresh **strawberries**
¼ cup fresh **blueberries**
¼ cup fresh **raspberries**
2 tablespoons **honey**
3 fresh **mint leaves**

***Note:** Choose containers with well-fitting lids for an on-the-go breakfast, lunch, or snack.*

1. Choose three (8-ounce) containers; these can be jars or bowls, glass, or plastic.*

2. Combine the graham cracker crumbs, butter, granola, sugar, poppy seeds, and coriander in a medium bowl.

3. Divide the mixture evenly between the three jars and press into the bottom to form a base.

4. Add the cream cheese, Greek yogurt, and vanilla extract to a medium bowl, stirring to combine.

5. Pour yogurt mixture over the graham cracker granola crust, cover with a lid or plastic wrap, and chill in the fridge overnight.

6. Before serving, top with the strawberries, blueberries, raspberries, honey, and mint.

NUTRITION	Per Serving	% of Daily Value
Calories	717	33%
Total Fat	49.38 g	102%
Saturated Fat	30.1 g	—
Polyunsaturated Fat	2.829 g	—
Monounsaturated Fat	13.658 g	—
Trans Fat	0.002 g	—
Cholesterol	117 mg	—
Sodium	438 mg	29%
Total Carbohydrates	62.04 g	25%
Dietary Fiber	3.3 g	13%
Total Sugars	50.47 g	—
Protein	10.84 g	20%
Vitamin A	1526 mcg	65%
Vitamin C	16.7 mcg	22%
Vitamin D	33 mcg	6%
Potassium	357 mg	8%
Calcium	184 mg	18%
Iron	2.48 mg	14%

Strawberry Coconut Yogurt

Prep time: 15 minutes
Cook time: 12 minutes
Total time: 27 minutes

LEVEL 2: EASY

. . . .

Bursting with flavor from the crunchy granola topping, tart strawberries, toasted coconut, and sweet honey, this is an easy dessert to whip up when you're in a time crunch. In fact, it may very well become your go-to dessert for busy nights.

. . . .

MAKES 4 SERVINGS

1 cup **unsweetened shredded coconut**
2 cups plain **Greek yogurt**
2 cups **granola**
2 cups chopped **strawberries**
4 tablespoons **honey**

1. Choose four (8-ounce) containers; these can be jars or bowls, glass, or plastic.*

2. Preheat oven to 325°F and line a cookie sheet with parchment paper.

3. Bake the shredded coconut on the prepared cookie sheet for 6 minutes. Toss and bake for an additional 6 minutes, or until golden brown.

4. Divide the yogurt evenly between the four bowls, add the granola, and top with the strawberries.

5. Sprinkle with the toasted coconut and drizzle with honey. Serve and enjoy!

*Note: Choose containers with well-fitting lids for an on-the-go breakfast, lunch, or snack.

NUTRITION	Per Recipe	% of Daily Value
Calories	770	35%
Total Fat	29.99 g	62%
Saturated Fat	19.401 g	—
Polyunsaturated Fat	3.159 g	—
Monounsaturated Fat	5.039 g	—
Trans Fat	—	—
Cholesterol	16 mg	—
Sodium	308 mg	21%
Total Carbohydrates	114.71 g	47%
Dietary Fiber	10 g	40%
Total Sugars	68.3 g	—
Protein	13.59 g	25%
Vitamin A	141 mcg	6%
Vitamin C	43.3 mcg	58%
Vitamin D	4 mcg	1%
Potassium	711 mg	15%
Calcium	210 mg	21%
Iron	2.53 mg	14%

Blueberry Yogurt Granola Jar

Prep time: 15 minutes
Cook time: 1 minute
Total time: 16 minutes

LEVEL 1: VERY EASY

. . . .

Yes, mustard seeds really are the secret Ingredient in this yogurt dessert! The seeds are toasted until fragrant, ground using a mortar and pestle, and sprinkled as the final touch on crunchy granola-topped creamy yogurt. If you prefer a subtle flavor, go for yellow seeds. If you want something more pungent, try brown or black ones!

. . . .

MAKES 4 SERVINGS

1 teaspoon **yellow mustard seeds**
1 cup **Greek yogurt**
½ cup **blueberries**
1 teaspoon **brown sugar**
1 cup **granola**

1. Choose four (8-ounce) containers; these can be jars or bowls, glass, or plastic.*

2. Cook the mustard seeds in a small, hot skillet set over medium-high heat, until fragrant (30–60 seconds). Transfer immediately to a mortar and pestle and grind the seeds into a fine powder. Set aside.

3. Combine the yogurt, blueberries, and sugar in a medium bowl, mixing well. Divide the mixture between the serving containers.

4. Top with the granola and a sprinkle of the powdered mustard seeds. Serve and enjoy!

***Note:** Choose containers with well-fitting lids for an on-the-go breakfast, lunch, or snack.*

NUTRITION	Per Serving	% of Daily Value
Calories	195	9%
Total Fat	6.44 g	9%
Saturated Fat	1.598 g	—
Polyunsaturated Fat	1.165 g	—
Monounsaturated Fat	3.298 g	—
Trans Fat	0.04 g	—
Cholesterol	7.108 mg	2%
Sodium	28.3 mg	2%
Total Carbohydrates	28.24 g	11%
Dietary Fiber	3.7 g	13%
Total Sugars	10.95 g	12%
Protein	8.1 g	16%
Vitamin A	76.5 mcg	3%
Vitamin C	2 mcg	3%
Vitamin D	1.7 mcg	0.25%
Potassium	101 mg	6%
Calcium	101 mg	10%
Iron	1 mg	6%

Index